The Hawai'i Garden
Tropical Shrubs

The Hawai'i Garden
Tropical Shrubs

HORACE F. CLAY and JAMES C. HUBBARD
photographs by RICK GOLT

University of Hawaii Press • Honolulu

First edition 1977
Paperback edition 1987

Copyright © 1977 by The University Press of Hawaii
All rights reserved
Manufactured in Singapore

Library of Congress Cataloging in Publication Data

Clay, Horace Freestone, 1918–
  The Hawai'i garden.

  Includes index.
  CONTENTS: 1. Tropical exotics.—2. Tropical shrubs.
  1. Gardening—Hawaii—Collected works. 2. Plants,
Ornamental—Hawaii—Collected works. 3. Tropical
plants—Hawaii—Collected works. 4. Landscape gardening
—Hawaii—Collected works. 5. Plants, Cultivated—
Hawaii—Collected works. I. Hubbard, James C., joint
author. II. Golt, R. S. III. Title.
SB453.2H3C55   635.9'09969   77-7363
ISBN 0-8248-0465-1 (v.1)
ISBN 0-8248-0466-X (v.2)

ISBN 0-8248-1128-3 (v.2 pbk)

The Hawai'i Garden volumes are dedicated to Elizabeth Loy McCandless Marks, who has worked selflessly and tirelessly to further the interests of tropical botany and horticulture in Hawai'i.

To Ellen Doubleday, whose love of books and gardening has led her to help in many ways to preserve and beautify America's gardens, this volume, *Tropical Shrubs,* is dedicated.

Contents

Contents

Preface

Tropical Shrubs and its companion volume, *Tropical Exotics,* are intended to serve as a guide for all Hawai'i's gardeners to the cultivation and enjoyment of the Islands' ornamental plants. Detailed information is given about each of the species chosen as outstanding examples of plants in specific categories: the species history and the origin of its name; how it grows, where it grows best, and its best use in the garden; how to propagate, prune, and fertilize it; and any serious disadvantages it may have as a garden plant.

Tropical Shrubs compiles information about Hawai'i's 103 most popular and most commonly used shrubby ornamentals. These plants, smaller than trees and larger than groundcovers, are generally grown as specimens or in mass plantings for hedges, borders, and container cultivation. They differ from those plants listed in *Tropical Exotics* in that they tend to be mostly woody in structure, whereas the exotics are mostly herbaceous and somewhat tender. The reader will find what at first glance appears to be glaring omissions from this book: Plants such as the common hedge materials mock orange *(Murraya paniculata),* privet *(Ligustrum lucidum),* and oleander *(Nerium indicum)* are not to be found in this book, because, in actuality, they are trees.

In order to make the information about each individual species as complete as possible, some repetition is unavoidable, particularly in discussions of closely related plants. To minimize such repetition, appendixes are added covering material that is generally applicable to the plants presented in this volume—detailed information on insect pests and plant diseases and their control, and plant propagation techniques.

Occasionally in the text the name of a plant will be seen printed in bold face type. This indicates that the plant thus set apart is fully described elsewhere in this volume.

A few words of explanation about the choice of photographs: The intention has been to depict each plant, not in the conventional, literal, ''whole plant'' style, but in an interpretative, symbolic, artistic manner. For the most part, the photographs concentrate on a small physical area of the subject, to create an image that is visually pleasing, but at the same time always true to the nature of the plant and expressive of its particular individuality.

Botanical nomenclature for families and genera follows that used in the seventh edition of *Willis' Dictionary of the Flowering Plants and Ferns,* edited by A. Shaw (1973). Botanist Dr. Derral Herbst has authenticated all species and varietal names in this volume. We greatly appreciate his careful work.

Much of the information on history and practical uses of the plants was obtained from three works: M. C. Neal, *In Gardens of Hawaii* (1965); J. C. Th. Uphoff, *Dictionary of Economic Plants,* 2nd ed. (1968); and I. H. Burkill, *A*

Dictionary of the Economic Products of the Malay Peninsula, 2nd ed. (1966).

For the meanings and origins of plant names we found particularly helpful *The Royal Horticultural Society Dictionary of Gardening,* edited by F. J. Chittenden, 2nd ed. (1956). Other useful references were R. S. Woods, *The Naturalist's Lexicon* (1944); L. H. Bailey, *How Plants Get Their Names* (1933); *Webster's New Collegiate Dictionary* (1976); and *The Encyclopedia Britannica,* 15th ed. (1976).

In addition to these sources, we have consulted many other works, including L. H. Bailey, *The Standard Cyclopedia of Horticulture* (1947), and *Manual of Cultivated Plants* (1949); *Curtis's Botanical Magazine* (1787–1975); A. Engler and K. Prantl, *Die natürlichen Pfanzenfamilien* (1887–1914); A. Graf, *Exoctica 3* (1976); *Index Londonensis* (1929 and supplements); *Index Kewensis* (1895 and supplements); *Paxton's Magazine of Botany* (1834–1849); P. C. Standley, *Trees and Shrubs of Mexico* (1920–1926); H. O'Gorman, *Mexican Flowing Trees and Plants* (1961); L. E. Bishop, *Honolulu Botanic Gardens Inventory, 1972* (1973); H. St. John, *List of the Flowering Plants in Hawaii* (1973); H. L. Li, *The Garden Flowers of China* (1959); F. Kitamura and Y. Ishizu, *Garden Plants in Japan* (1963); C. Letty, *Wild Flowers of the Transvaal* (1962); M. Hulme, *Wild Flowers of Natal* (1954); R. B. Streets, *The Diagnosis of Plant Diseases* (1969); C. L. Metcalf and W. P. Flint, *Destructive and Useful Insects,* 4th ed. (1962); H. T. Hartmann and D. E. Kester, *Plant Propagation: Principles and Practices,* 3rd ed. (1975); and Staff of the L. H. Bailey Hortorium, *Hortus Third* (1976).

Acknowledgments

We wish to express our very deep appreciation for the generous financial help and unfailing cooperation extended by the Stanley Smith Horticultural Trust, the Bradley L. Geist and Victoria S. Geist Foundation, Elizabeth Loy McCandless Marks, Ellen Doubleday, Laura Nott Dowsett, Dorothy Bading Lanquist, and Mr. and Mrs. Alfred J. Ostheimer III.

Our thanks go also to Mr. John Gregg Allerton, Dr. John W. Beardsley, Mrs. Lillian Craig, Mr. John K. Hayasaka, Dr. and Mrs. William John Holmes, Mr. and Mrs. John T. Humme, Mr. and Mrs. Tamotsu Kubota, Ms. Linda G. Lee, Mrs. Boyd MacNaughton, Mr. Albert P. Martinez, Mr. J. L. Merkel, Dr. Wallace C. Mitchell, Dr. Harold St. John, Mr. Hiroshi Tagami and Mr. Richard Hart, Mrs. H. Alexander Walker, Mr. Paul R. Weissich, and Mr. and Mrs. Warren Q. K. Yee.

For encouragment and assistance of many kinds we are also deeply indebted to the Friends of Foster Garden, Harold L. Lyon Arboretum, Honolulu Academy of Arts, Honolulu Board of Water Supply, Honolulu Botanic Gardens, the Garden Club of Honolulu, the Outdoor Circle, the Bernice P. Bishop Museum library, the Hawaii State Library, and the libaries of the University of Hawaii.

A Word of Caution

Do Not Eat or Taste Parts of Unfamiliar Plants

Plants have been used since time beyond measure both as foods and as medicines. In many cases, the plants are benign agents, producing little or no ill effect when they are eaten—and often they are credited with doing much good. Many plants, however, are very irritating to the body's tissues, internally or externally, and in some cases can cause severe sickness or death. The bits of information about uses as medicines and foods offered in these books are included only because of their historic interest. This mention must not be construed as being a recommendation for their use as foods or medicines. Often, highly poisonous plants must be thoroughly processed before their toxic properties are removed, making them safe to use. Failure to prepare plants properly may lead quickly to illness or death.

The general rule, when encountering unknown plants is this: *Do not eat or taste any part of any unfamiliar plant.* Many of Hawai'i's garden plants, including some of those listed in these books, contain irritating or poisonous agents that may be highly detrimental to the user. Never apply parts of unknown plants to the skin or eyes or mouth, and never eat them. Many age-old remedies based upon tropical plants are beneficial, but often their worthwhile attributes are based upon how and when and in what state of preparation they are used. The uninformed person should never try these remedies.

Modern scientists are studying ancient folk remedies to determine whether beneficial medicines can be obtained from them. Until the plants are tested adequately, however, the home medicine chest and the family menu should not include any unfamiliar plants.

The Hawai'i Garden
Tropical Shrubs

Piperaceae
(Pepper Family)

The name Piperaceae is derived from *piper,* the Latin word for pepper. The pepper family consists of four genera and about 2,000 species from throughout the earth's tropics. Plants in the family are mainly shrubs, vines, or trees. Probably the most valuable of the species is *Piper nigrum,* a vine that produces two commercial condiments, black and white pepper. Two other peppers are important mainly to the peoples of tropical Asia and the Pacific islands; they are the betel pepper vine *(P. betle),* the leaves of which are chewed with baked coral lime and the nut of the betel palm *(Areca catechu),* and the 'awa shrub *(Piper methysticum)* whose roots are the source of the soporific ceremonial drink, 'awa.

The peperomias, a large and very interesting plant group in themselves, were formerly classified as members of the Piperaceae; currently they are placed in a separate family, Peperomiaceae. Chili peppers and bell peppers (*Capsicum annuum* cultivars) are not true peppers at all, but are members of the **tomato family (Solanaceae).**

Piper magnificum
Peruvian Pepper

This Peruvian native is a highly ornamental relative of the three more mundane but constantly used pepper species—commercial pepper *(Piper nigrum)*, 'awa *(P. methysticum),* and betel pepper *(P. betle)*. Several ornamental peppers have been introduced into Hawai'i's horticulture in recent years. Like the Peruvian pepper, these species are grown for their colorful foliage.

The Peruvian pepper is an exquisitely beautiful plant. Its large leaves —glistening, dark green upper surfaces and brilliant burgundy undersides— exhibit high color in shaded garden plantings. Superficially, the shrub resembles several of the larger-leaved **panax (*Polyscias* spp.)**. Its delicate foliage and flowers set it apart from the panax, however; the plant is extremely sun sensitive and will not tolerate exposed conditions, as the panax will. With protective care, the Peruvian pepper will flourish as a garden specimen or as a container plant.

Piper is the Latin name for the pepper of commerce; *magnificum,* meaning great and noble, refers to the plant's royally endowed leaves.

HABIT	An erect, woody, evergreen shrub that grows to about 9 feet in height; the plant is stiffly vertical; trunk and branches covered with heavy layers of thick bark; new branches exhibit small, corky, winged protrusions along their square stems. Glistening, rounded and pleated leaves, about 8 inches long, are dark metallic green on upper surfaces and brilliant burgundy beneath; each leaf marked by a strong white midrib. Clusters of light green, tubular flowers, about 3 inches in length, hang from longer burgundy stems. Flowers are followed by insignificant, black, pepper-like berries. Moderate growth rate; easily transplanted.
GROWING CONDITIONS	Cannot tolerate full sunshine; grows best in cool, moist, partially shaded locations, in rich, well-composted, well-watered, well-drained soil. In areas where cloud cover is considerable and fairly constant, the shrub may be set out in less shaded locations.
USE	Specimen plant; mass planting; container plant; colorful, tropical foliage.
PROPAGATION	By cuttings or seeds.
INSECTS/DISEASES	None of any significance in Hawai'i.
PRUNING	Remove dead, damaged, or straggly branches and leaves.
FERTILIZING	Apply general garden fertilizer (10-30-10) to the planting bed at 3-month intervals, and to container plants at monthly intervals. Water immediately and thoroughly after each application.
DISADVANTAGES	Plant will sunburn easily.

Moraceae
(Fig Family)

The fig family's scientific name comes from *morus,* the Latin word for the mulberries, some of this group's more tasty and succulent fruits. The family consists of 53 genera and about 1,400 species, most of which are native to the earth's tropical and subtropical regions. Among the edible fruits are the fig of commerce *(Ficus carica),* mulberry *(Morus nigra* and *M. alba),* bread-fruit *(Artocarpus altilis),* and jakfruit *(A. heterophyllus).* Marijuana *(Cannabis sativa)* and hops *(Humulus lupulus)* were formerly considered members of the fig family but are now placed in a separate family, Cannabidaceae. Hawaiians and other Pacific peoples have beaten their tapas from the bark of the paper mulberry *(Broussonetia papyrifera)* for centuries. The great banyans and other fig trees *(Ficus* spp.) comprise a major portion of this important family. In Asia the most revered fig is the sacred bo *(F. religiosa),* for it was while sitting beneath a bo tree that the Lord Buddha received enlightenment.

The **mistletoe fig *(F. diversifolia)*** is the only member of this highly diversified family that is widely used as an ornamental shrub in Hawaiian gardens. Several fig giants are often planted in containers, however, and used as shrub-size specimens. These include the rubber plant *(F. elastica),* the Chinese banyan *(F. retusa),* and the benjamin banyan *(F. benjamina).*

Ficus diversifolia
Mistletoe Fig, Cherry Banyan

This charming fig is native to the mountain forests of Malaysia, where it grows epiphytically on trees. Unlike its parasitic namesake, the mistletoe (*Phoradendron* spp.), the mistletoe fig does not take its nourishment from the host tree on which it grows. Although, as an epiphyte, the plant requires only small amounts of organic material, it can easily adapt to the growth conditions of regular garden soil, where it is usually planted.

Gardeners appreciate the mistletoe fig for its crisp appearance, small size, tidiness, and graceful habit. It is often found in Oriental-style gardens, and is also one of Hawai'i's most successfully grown container plants. Mistletoe fig can be allowed to develop naturally or it can be clipped and trained into loosely regimented forms. It prefers the shade; leaves are dark green in sun-sheltered areas, lighter, more chartreuse in sunnier areas.

Ficus is the Latin name for both the edible fig tree and its fruit; *diversifolia*, from *divers,* meaning varied, and *folium,* meaning a leaf, refers to the considerable variety of foliage forms. The plant's superficial resemblance to the American mistletoe is responsible for its most commonly used name. It is called the cherry banyan because of its tiny, cherry-colored fruits.

HABIT — An erect, woody, evergreen shrub that grows to about 4 feet in height; it has a loose, angular, flexible branching system and an open crown. The variously shaped, leathery, olive-green upper leaves are dotted with tiny white spots; all leaves have rust-colored undersides. Small, pear-shaped, green-turning-to red figs, about ¼ inch in diameter, are attached by long stems along the branches; these fruits appear continuously throughout the year. As with other figs, flower parts are found within the fruit. Fruit and stems contain a sticky, milky sap. Slow growth rate; easily transplanted.

GROWING CONDITIONS — Very adaptable; will grow in full sun or partial shade, in scanty or rich soil. Grows best with constant moisture around the roots. Best foliage color is produced in partial shade. An excellent house plant, but languishes under salty conditions.

USE — Specimen plant; mass planting; container plant; bonsai.

PROPAGATION — Seeds are not viable in Hawai'i; however, the plant is easily grown from cuttings.

INSECTS/DISEASES — For scale, apply malathion or summer oil. For thrips and mealybugs, use diazinon. Roots are very susceptible to nematode infestation; this condition may be avoided by growing plant in sterilized soil. If an older plant becomes infested with nematodes, take new cuttings from healthy branches and destroy the parent.

PRUNING — Naturally tidy but accepts judicious pruning; can be easily and attractively shaped. Strong but limber branches permit training into upright or cascading forms.

FERTILIZING — Apply general garden fertilizer (10-30-10) to the planting bed at 3-month intervals, to plants in containers at monthly intervals. Water immediately and thoroughly.

DISADVANTAGES — Plant is highly susceptible to nematode infestation.

Polygonaceae
(Buckwheat Family)

The term Polygonaceae comes from the Greek word *polygonos,* meaning many-jointed. This appellation accurately describes the knobbed stem structures of many members of the buckwheat family. Most of the plants in the family are found in the North Temperate Zone. The **ribbon bush (Homalocladium platycladum)** is one of the few tropical species. Most buckwheats are herbs; however, a few shrubs and a smaller number of trees belong to the group. The family's most useful and best known members are buckwheat *(Fagopyrum esculentum),* rhubarb *(Rheum rhaponticum),* sweetheart vine *(Antigonon leptopus),* and sea grape *(Coccoloba uvifera).*

Homalocladium platycladum
Ribbon Bush, Tapeworm Plant, Centipede Plant, Alupihan

The ribbon bush is a plant that ants like and that likes ants. Some of the ribbon bush's older stems are hollow cylinders. In the Solomon Islands, these natural apartments provide certain kinds of ants with protected living space. In return, the ants act as a protecting army, warding off destructive pests.

The vast majority of stems, however, are almost paper-flat, with no interior space, the characteristic that gives the shrub its descriptive vernacular names. The ribbon-like stems, vividly marked at the nodes, suggest the appearance of segmented tapeworms. Occasionally, when the short-lived leaves are still on the stems, the effect is that of many green-legged centipedes.

The ribbon bush is a graceful, tender plant, almost a succulent. Its appearance is quite similar to that of a fern or asparagus. Although most of the plant is leafless, its small arrow-shaped leaves can be found on the new stem growth. These leaves fall quickly from the maturing stems, which thereafter must perform most of the photosynthetic work done by foliage in other plants. The brilliant red fruits that occasionally form along the edges of the stems, give the shrub a festive, decorated appearance.

The plant is happiest in hot, humid locations and grows well in dark, shaded areas where its brilliant, light green color brightens the gloom.

Homalocladium, from the Greek words *homalos,* meaning smooth, and *klados,* meaning branch, refers to the satin-smooth stems; *platycladum,* from *platy,* meaning broad, and *klados,* meaning branch, refers to the stem's relative flatness. Filipinos sometimes call the ribbon bush by its Tagalog name, alupihan (centipede).

HABIT — A herbaceous, mounding shrub that grows to about 8 feet in Hawai'i, and to about 12 feet in the more humid tropics. Succulent, arching branches form an open crown. Flattened, leaflike stems bear sparsely spaced, arrowhead-shaped, light green leaves about 2 inches long; leaves appear on new growth but fall soon after formation. Insignificant white flowers appear in clusters at edges of stem joints. Attractive purple to red fruits, about ⅛ inch in diameter, occasionally follow the flowers. Moderate growth rate; easily transplanted.

GROWING CONDITIONS — Adaptable but prefers humid areas; will grow in areas of full sun or partial shade. Requires rich, well-drained soil with constant ground moisture. Not a beach plant.

USE — Specimen plant; container plant.

PROPAGATION — The plant is grown easily from cuttings but may also be propagated by seeds.

INSECTS/DISEASES — Relatively insect free in Hawai'i.

PRUNING — May be pruned severely to control size and shape; rejuvenates rapidly after pruning.

FERTILIZING — Apply general garden fertilizer (10-30-10) to the planting bed at 3-month intervals, to container plants monthly. Water immediately and thoroughly each time.

DISADVANTAGES — Requires more moisture than is naturally available in most gardens.

Nandinaceae
(Nandina Family)

The term Nandinaceae is derived from the word *nanten,* the Japanese name for the **heavenly bamboo *(Nandina domestica).*** It ranks as one of the smallest families in the plant kingdom, because its membership is limited to one species. Formerly, botanists included the plant in the better-known barberry family (Berberidaceae), two of whose members, barberry *(Berberis vulgaris)* and Oregon grape *(Mahonia aquifolium),* are oftentimes planted in North Temperate gardens.

Heavenly bamboo has been grown as a garden ornamental for a thousand years and more. Although it is unique botanically, there is much variation within the species. Many horticultural types have been developed over the centuries. Most of today's varieties, about 30 in number, have been developed from seeds in Japan. In size the plant ranges from dwarf to good-sized plants, and many foliar forms and color variations are grown. Heavenly bamboo's graceful foliage turns to rich autumn reds and golds in colder climates. In Hawai'i the foliage is induced to color in full sunlight. Plants set out in shady garden areas will develop delicate green leaves.

Nandina domestica
Heavenly Bamboo, T'ien Chu, Nanten, Sacred Bamboo

It is not a bamboo, but to the people in its native China and Japan it has a celestial relationship to that giant grass. "Heavenly bamboo" is a translation of both the Chinese name, t'ien chu, and the Japanese, nanten. In China the leafy canes of t'ien chu are often used in sacred observances, and some Chinese drink a decoction of the boiled stems as a tonic and as an aid to keeping young.

Nanten is a symbol of good fortune to the Japanese; many homes display the graceful plant at the left side of the entranceway. For the New Year, stalks of nanten are arranged with branches of pine and canes of bamboo as symbols of long life. Nanten wood, strong and straight, is fashioned into chopsticks and canes. Children are taught to eat using such chopsticks because the wood is said to help ward off illness. Also in Japan the dried fruit is processed into a cough medicine.

Nandina is the latinized form of nanten; *domestica* means belonging to the house or family.

HABIT
An erect, woody, evergreen shrub from 1 foot or less to about 15 feet in height, depending on horticultural variety. Multiple, bare, canelike stems are topped by a loose, airy crown of small, multicolored, bamboo-like leaves. The foliage differs considerably according to variety. White, cone-shaped flower clusters are followed by pendent, terra-cotta, ¼-inch berries. Moderate growth rate; easily transplanted.

GROWING CONDITIONS
Very adaptable; although originally from a colder, temperate climate, the plant will grow almost anywhere in Hawai'i, even at the beach if protected from salt winds. Requires rich, well-watered, well-drained soil; grows well in full sun or in shade.

USE
Specimen plant; mass planting; container plant; colorful foliage, flowers, and fruit.

PROPAGATION
Established varieties are propagated by root division or by cuttings; new varieties are propagated by seed. To divide at the root, remove and replant new cane after it has become semiwoody; if the cane, separated at the base, does not have established roots, it will develop new ones readily. Seeds must be refrigerated before they will germinate: first remove the fleshy covering; cover seeds in dampened, salt-free sand in a tightly covered container such as a pill bottle; store container in kitchen refrigerator for approximately 75 days; do not freeze. After refrigeration, plant out.

INSECTS/DISEASES
For scale, apply summer oil or malathion. For thrips, use diazinon or malathion.

PRUNING
Remove dead or damaged canes to below affected area; new foliage will sprout near tops of cut canes that are healthy. Easily trained to desired height and form.

FERTILIZING
Apply general garden fertilizer (10-30-10) to the planting bed at 3-month intervals, to container plants monthly. Plants sometimes exhibit brown-tipped or yellow leaves, which may indicate a lack of phosphorus, potash, or minor elements; apply 10-20-20 fertilizers supplemented with minor elements.

DISADVANTAGES
None.

14

Hydrangeaceae
(Hydrangea Family)

Hydrangeas formerly were classified as members of the saxifrage family (Saxifragaceae). Today, botanists have separated the hydrangeas from the saxifrages and established the family Hydrangeaceae. The name is derived from the Greek words, *hydor,* meaning water, and *angeion,* meaning vessel, in reference to the cup-shaped fruits produced by members of the group. Ten genera and about 115 species are included within the family. Being native to the North Temperate Zone and to South America's Andean uplands, most hydrangeas prefer cool locations. The majority are shrubs or small trees, very few are vines or herbs.

Hydrangea macrophylla, the common potted hydrangea of the florists' trade, is commercially the most important family member. Indeed, its use is strictly ornamental, although a close relative, the tree hydrangea or sachalin *(Hydrangea paniculata),* has fine-grained wood which is used in Japan for making umbrella handles, canes, tobacco pipes, and pegs. The leaves of another Japanese relative, *H. thunbergii* var. *thunbergii,* are dried and processed into *ama-cha,* a sweet tea.

Well-known near-relatives in the saxifrage family include wild gooseberry *(Grossularia hirtella),* garden currant *(G. sativa),* and coral bells *(Heuchera sanguinea).* The strawberry begonia *(Saxifraga sarmentosa)*—which is neither a strawberry nor a begonia—and mock orange *(Philadelphus coronarius)*—which should not be confused with *Murraya paniculata,* another plant commonly known in Hawai'i as mock orange—are also members of the saxifrage family.

Hydrangea macrophylla var. *thunbergii*

Japanese Hydrangea, Ajisai, Bigleaf Hydrangea, Pōpō Hau, Hortensia, Mil Flores

Many named horticultural varieties of the Japanese hydrangea are recognized, for the plant has been propagated in Oriental and Occidental gardens for many generations. In China, hydrangea culture reached its peak during the Sung Dynasty (A.D. 960–1280). Hydrangeas were introduced into England —and to Western horticulture—in 1790.

The native Japanese hydrangea's flower normally is pink. Blue flowers are produced artificially by applying considerable amounts of aluminum sulfate to the planting bed before buds form. Potted stock is induced to flower through forcing, being put first into cold boxes, then brought out into warm temperatures. An unusual characteristic is the fact that the tiny budlike flowerlets, almost invisible in the flower cluster, are the fertile blossoms, although they rarely produce seeds; the showier blossoms are always sterile.

Hydrangea, from *hydor,* water, and *angeion,* vessel, refers to the plant's cup-shaped fruits; *macrophyllum* comes from *makro-,* large, and *phyllon,* leaf; *thunbergii* is named for Dr. Karl Pehr Thunberg (1743–1828), professor of botany at Uppsala, Sweden. Hawaiians call the plant pōpō hau (snowball). The English name, hortensia, recalls an older botanical name. The Spanish term, mil flores (one thousand flowers), alludes to the myriad blossoms in each cluster.

HABIT A sprawling, woody, evergreen shrub that grows to about 8 feet in height in Hawai'i's cool uplands; dwarfed at lower elevations, growing only to about 2 feet. Soft young branches are covered with large, smooth leaves about 6 inches in diameter. Compact flower clusters, about 8 inches in diameter, appear in late fall and winter. Rarely produces seed in Hawai'i. Moderate growth rate; easily transplanted.

GROWING CONDITIONS Prefers cool, moist, shaded or partially shaded areas above the 2,000-foot level in Hawai'i, but will grow with varying degrees of success at lower elevations. In acid rain-forest soil, the flowers are blue; in the more alkaline Island soils, they are pink. Plants require rich, well-watered, well-drained soil.

USE Specimen plant; mass planting; container plant; colorful flowers.

PROPAGATION Generally by cuttings.

INSECTS/DISEASES For leaf spot disease, apply captan. For powdery mildew, use dried powdered sulfur or liquid mildew fungicide.

PRUNING May be pruned severely to shape and to induce new growth and flowering.

FERTILIZING Apply general garden fertilizer high in phosphorus and potassium (10-20-20) to the planting bed at 3-month intervals, to container plants monthly. Apply 1 teaspoon aluminum sulfate to soil around each plant at monthly intervals to produce blue flowers, or 1 teaspoon calcium carbonate (agricultural lime) to insure pink flowers.

DISADVANTAGE Not a good plant to use in warm lowlands and beach areas.

Pittosporaceae
(Pittosporum Family)

The name *Pittosporum* is derived from the Latin *pix,* meaning pitch, and Greek *sporos,* meaning seed; many members of this family produce sticky black seeds. There are nine genera within this small family (*Billardiera, Marianthus, Sollya,* and others), eight of which are native only to the island continent of Australia. The ninth genus, *Pittosporum,* is found in tropical and subtropical Africa, Australia, New Zealand, Asia, and the Pacific islands. Three quarters of the 200 or so species in the family belong to this genus.

The family Pittosporaceae consists primarily of tropical trees and shrubs, some of which contain large amounts of resin in the inner parts of the bark. Twenty-three species of native Hawaiian pittosporums are recognized. Hawaiians, who gave the generic name hōʻawa to all Island species, have used the fruits of some in the treatment of body sores. The most popular Hawaiian garden species is *Pittosporum hosmeri* var. *longifolium,* a native of the Kona and Kaʻū districts on the Big Island. This plant's seeds form a part of the diet of the Hawaiian crow (ʻalalā).

The Japanese native, *P. tobira,* is the most commonly used family member in Hawaiian gardens; its cultivar **'Wheeler's Dwarf'** is rapidly gaining wide acceptance into Island horticulture. A colorful relative used extensively in Southern California gardens, as either a vine or a shrub, is an Australian native, the bluebell creeper, *Sollya heterophylla.*

Pittosporum tobira cv. 'Wheeler's Dwarf'
Dwarf Pittosporum

One of Hawai'i's most common landscape plants is *Pittosporum tobira,* a tree from the temperate regions of Asia which generally is pruned into hedge and shrub shapes in the garden. A cultivar of this plant, developed from a chance seedling among thousands being grown for the purpose of finding a new form, was introduced into the nursery trade in 1969. The seedling, 'Wheeler's Dwarf,' was propagated by Carl Wheeler, Central Georgia Nursery, Macon. Since its introduction, the plant has spread rapidly into ornamental use. It was first brought to Hawai'i in 1970.

The dwarf's chief attributes are its always handsome foliage, slow growth habit, low maintenance requirements, and especially, its compact form. Whereas its parent grows easily into a 35-foot tree, the oldest dwarf has attained a height of only 3 feet. The plant's mature leaves are a rich dark green, somewhat the color of the parent's; its new growth is a shining, brilliant lime-green. Its best use in the garden is as a specimen plant for rockeries, mass groundcover material, or a tidy container plant.

The name *Pittosporum,* from *pix,* meaning pitch, and *sporos,* meaning seed, describes the sticky fruits found on many members of the family; *tobira* stems from tobera, the Japanese name for the species.

HABIT A low, mounding, woody, evergreen shrub that grows to about 3 feet in height. Glossy, dark green leaves about 3 inches long grow in whorls around stiff woody stems. This cultivar has not been known to flower and fruit in Hawai'i. Moderate growth rate; easily transplanted.

GROWING CONDITIONS Very adaptable; will grow nearly everywhere, even at the beach except in extreme salt conditions; prefers rich, well-watered, well-drained soil. Best foliar growth is produced in full sunny locations.

USE Specimen plant; mass planting; container plant.

PROPAGATION Grown from cuttings.

INSECTS/DISEASES For scale, apply malathion or summer oil. For spider mites, use wettable sulfur.

PRUNING Prune lightly to remove unsightly or unattractive branches. The plant is naturally dome-shaped and densely foliaged, needs little pruning.

FERTILIZING Apply general garden fertilizer (10-30-10) to the planting bed at 3-month intervals, and to container plants at monthly intervals. Water immediately and thoroughly after each application. At times the plant may exhibit abnormally yellow leaves; in that event, apply fertilizers containing trace elements at monthly intervals until condition is corrected.

DISADVANTAGES None.

Rosaceae
(Rose Family)

According to Sappho, the poetess of Lesbos, the rose is the Queen of Flowers. If that be so, then certainly Rosaceae is one of the royal families of the plant kingdom. More than 100 genera and 2,000 species are included in the family.

Both Herodotus, the "father of history," and Pliny, writing in his *Natural History*, mentioned the cultural and horticultural values of roses. Most relatives of roses are trees, shrubs, or herbs; only a very few are vines. Ornamental relatives include bridal wreath *(Spiraea prunifolia)*, cotoneaster *(Cotoneaster pannosa)*, and firethorn *(Pyracantha angustifolia)*. The fruiting relatives are even more important than the ornamentals. These include strawberry *(Fragaria × ananassa)*, raspberry and blackberry *(Rubus* spp.), apple *(Malus pumila)*, pear *(Pyrus communis)*, and loquat *(Eriobotrya japonica)*.

Native Hawaiian relatives are 'ūlei *(Osteomeles anthyllidifolia)*, whose strong wood was used for making fish spears and the hoops of fishnets, and 'ākala *(Rubus macraei* and *R. hawaiiensis)*, the wild Hawaiian raspberries.

The family takes its name from *rosa*, the Latin word for rose.

Rhaphiolepis umbellata f. *ovata*
Yeddo Hawthorn, Sharinbai, Kokutan

The Yeddo hawthorn is a botanical variant that originated in the temperate parts of Asia. Its wild parent, *Rhaphiolepis umbellata,* is found throughout the warmer regions of Korea and Japan. It is seldom if ever used as a landscape plant.

In Japan the bark of the Yeddo hawthorn yields an excellent brown dye for the coloring of *tsumugi,* a fine silk pongee used for kimonos and similar apparel. In Japan the plant is called sharinbai (spokes of a wheel, referring to the arrangement of the leaves on the stems), but in Hawai'i its Okinawan name is kokutan, which is also the name of a Ryukyu Island look-alike. Yeddo is a variant spelling of Edo, the old name for Tōkyō.

The Yeddo hawthorn is a slow-growing, constantly blooming shrub that is much used in Hawai'i. Its graceful, structured habit is equally at home in traditional Oriental or in contemporary Hawaiian gardens.

Rhaphiolepis, from *rhaphis,* meaning needle, and *lepis,* meaning a scale, refers to the tiny needle-shaped flower bracts; *umbellata,* describes the umbel-shaped, or rounded, flower clusters; *ovata,* meaning egg-shaped, describes the distinctive oval leaves.

HABIT An erect, spreading, woody, evergreen shrub that grows to about 8 feet in height. Usually has a short central trunk with several attractively spreading branches and a dense foliar crown. Leathery, oval, smooth-edged leaves, 1 to 2 inches long, are borne in thick clusters at irregular intervals along the branches; leaves have glossy, dark green upper surfaces and lighter, duller, gray-green undersides. Fragrant small white flowers, about ½ inch in diameter, form in raised clusters above the leaves; they appear during much of the year, especially in the cool months. Spherical blue-black fruits, about ⅓ inch in diameter. Flower and fruit clusters usually appear simultaneously on the plant throughout the year. Slow growth rate; easily transplanted.

GROWING CONDITIONS Very adaptable; grows nearly everywhere, even at the beach if protected from severe salt conditions; grows well in full sun or partial shade. Although hardy and able to withstand considerable inattention, does best when planted in rich, well-watered, well-drained soil and given regular care.

USE Specimen plant; mass planting; informal hedging; container plant; colorful, fragrant flowers, and attractive fruit; bonsai specimen.

PROPAGATION Grown generally from seeds or cuttings.

INSECTS/DISEASES For scale, apply malathion or summer oil. For thrips, use diazinon or malathion.

PRUNING Highly adaptable to extensive pruning and to shaping into regimented forms; easily pruned and trained to cascade over a container's rim.

FERTILIZING Apply general garden fertilizer (10-30-10) to the planting bed at 3-month intervals, and to container plants at monthly intervals. Water immediately and thoroughly.

DISADVANTAGES None.

Rhaphiolepis × delacourii
Enchantress Hawthorn

This is one of several horticultural hybrids of *Rhaphiolepis* that have been developed in the nursery trade through hybridization of two common species, **Yeddo hawthorn** *(R. umbellata)* and Indian hawthorn (*R. indica*). It was developed at the Delacour Nursery in Cannes, France, in 1896. Several California nurseries currently produce the hybrid under its patented name, Enchantress. As a patented hybrid, the plant cannot be reproduced commercially without the permission of the patent holder.

Enchantress hawthorn differs from its parents in that its flowers are a deep pink. Those of the Yeddo hawthorn are white, and those of the Indian hawthorn are pale pink. Enchantress flowers have a slight fragrance derived from the hybrid's Japanese parent, while the color of the flowers and the notched leaves come from its Chinese ancestor.

Rhaphiolepis, from *rhaphis*, meaning needle, and *lepis*, meaning a scale, refers to the tiny needle-shaped flower bracts; *umbellata*, the species name of one parent, describes the umbel-shaped, or rounded, flower clusters; *indica* refers to the other parent's native habitat, China. (Linnaeus used the word *indica* for both India and China.)

HABIT	An erect, spreading, woody, evergreen shrub that grows to about 6 feet. Usually has a short central trunk with several picturesquely spreading branches and a dense foliar crown. Leathery, oval, leaves, 1 to 2 inches long, are borne in thick clusters at irregular intervals along the branches; leaves are more pointed than are those of *R. umbellata* and have distinctive notches along their edges; they are glossy dark green on upper surfaces and lighter, duller gray-green on the undersides. Airy clusters of fragrant, small, rose-pink flowers. Spherical, blue-black fruits, about ⅓ inch in diameter, follow the blossoms. Flower and fruit clusters usually appear simultaneously on the plant throughout the year. Slow growth rate; easily transplanted.
GROWING CONDITIONS	Very adaptable; grows nearly everywhere in Hawai'i, even at the beach if protected from severe salt conditions; grows well in full sun or partial shade. Although hardy and able to withstand some inattention, does best when planted in rich, well-watered, well-drained soil and given regular care.
USE	Specimen plant; mass planting; informal hedging; container plant; colorful, fragrant flowers, and attractive fruits.
PROPAGATION	Can be propagated only from cuttings (sometimes by airlayering or grafting); seeds would produce variable offspring.
INSECTS/DISEASES	For scale, apply malathion or summer oil. For thrips, use diazinon or malathion.
PRUNING	Highly adaptable to substantial pruning in order to obtain special shapes or bonsai forms; easily pruned and trained to cascade over the sides of containers.
FERTILIZING	Apply general garden fertilizer (10-30-10) to the planting bed at 3-month intervals, to container plants monthly. Water immediately and thoroughly each time.
DISADVANTAGES	None.

Rosa chinensis var. *viridiflora*

Green Rose, Loke Lau

This very unusual rose is native to Central China, where for centuries its more colorful ancestor, the Chinese rose *(Rosa chinensis),* has been used by horticulturists as breeding stock for many spectacular hybrids. The Chinese call the parent plant yüeh chi, meaning monthly rose, because of its ability to bloom continuously during the months-long growing season. In Hawai‘i the loke lau, or green rose, produces narrow green bracts in tight, flower-like clusters.

The hybrid tea roses are derived from Chinese rose stock, the first of which was imported into England in 1768, where they were crossed with European roses. The Chinese rose and the climbing rose *(R. multiflora)* are the parents of the polyanthus hybrids, the small, fragrant, many-flowered plants popularly grown in today's gardens. Another relative, native to the Mideast, is the damask rose *(R. damascena).* In Hawai‘i it is the much-loved loke lani, heavenly rose, the official flower of the island of Maui.

The Chinese have several uses for *R. chinensis.* An ointment prepared from the fruits is applied to wounds, sprains, and other injuries. The dried flower petals scent teas and flavor food. "Dew of Roses," a cooling summer drink; rose water, the well-known cologne; and attar of roses, the oil that rises to the top of rose water, are all derived from the fragrant petals.

Rosa is the Latin name for several members of the rose family; *chinensis* refers to this species' native habitat; *viridiflora* means green flower.

HABIT An erect, woody, evergreen shrub that grows to about 6 feet in height; multiple, bare, woody stems have a few thorns. Has a loose, open crown of glossy, dark green, narrow leaflets. What we call the "flower" actually has no petals, but is composed entirely of frilly modified leaves, or bracts, densely packed; some may be about 2 inches in diameter. A newly opened "flower" is light green in color; as it ages, it darkens to a deeper green. They last for a long time because the bracts are sturdier tissue than the more usual delicate flower petals. The flowers are sterile, lacking reproductive parts. Moderate growth rate; easily transplanted.

GROWING CONDITIONS Very adaptable, will grow almost anywhere except in sandy or salty locations. Although essentially a temperate climate plant, it grows well in Hawai‘i. It requires rich, well-watered, well-drained soil, and "blooms" best in full sunny locations.

USE Specimen plant; curiosity.

PROPAGATION Propagated by cuttings from either the soft green tips or from semiwoody stems.

INSECTS/DISEASES For Chinese rose beetles, use one of the residual insecticides, such as carbaryl.

PRUNING Prune to remove dead or damaged wood; weak stems and branches should always be removed. The plant may be pruned severely to induce new growth and flowering.

FERTILIZING Apply high phosphorous and potash fertilizer (10-20-20) at 4-month intervals.

DISADVANTAGES May be savagely attacked by Chinese rose beetles.

Leguminosae
(Bean Family)

The bean family is one of the great groups of food and fodder plants. It includes four of mankind's most important seed crops—peas (*Pisum* spp.), beans (*Phaseolus* spp.), soybeans *(Glycine soja)*, and peanuts *(Arachis hypogaea)*. Important fodder crops are alfalfa *(Medicago sativa)*, the clovers (*Trifolium* spp.), and the vetches (*Vicia* spp.). The natural blue dye, indigo, is produced by several plants in the genus *Indigofera*.

The bean family is so large and widespread (having more than 600 genera and 12,000 species) that botanists have divided it into three subfamilies, the Mimosoideae (mimosas), Caesalpinioideae (sennas), and Papilionoideae (peas). In Hawai'i the mimosas include the native koa *(Acacia koa)*, opiuma *(Pithecellobium dulce)*, monkeypod *(Samanea saman)*, powderpuff plant *(Calliandra inaequilatera)*, and kiawe *(Prosopis pallida)*. The sennas include tamarind *(Tamarindus indica)*, the several orchid trees (*Bauhinia* spp.), the many kinds of shower trees (*Cassia* spp.), and royal poinciana *(Delonix regia)*. The peas include the agricultural crops listed above as well as many other species, such as the native Hawaiian wiliwili *(Erythrina sandwicensis)*. These subfamilies are distinguished according to the kinds of flowers the plants produce: the mimosas have powderpuff-like flowers; the sennas have five-petaled orchid-like flowers; and the peas, boat-shaped flowers like those of sweet peas.

Caesalpinia pulcherrima f. *flava*
Yellow Pride of Barbados, Caballero, Peacock Flower,
'Ohai ali'i

The yellow pride of Barbados and its red-flowered parent *(Caesalpinia pulcherrima* f. *pulcherrima)*, probably are native to tropical America. In Mexico, where the plant is called caballero (cavalier), it is an important source of several dyes—red and brown dyes from the fruits and a red dye from the roots. Seeds contain gallic and tannic acids. A mouthwash is prepared from flowers and leaves in Mexico, and an eyewash from the flowers. Powdered flowers are said to be a good insecticide. In Guatemala the leaves are used to stupefy fish.

In India the plants are considered sacred by Hindus, who associate them with the god Shiva. Indians make ink from the charred wood. The powdered roots are used to treat convulsions in babies; flowers yield a remedy for intestinal worms; and the leaves are used as a purgative and to relieve fevers. Thais use the powdered seeds to treat stomachache. Indonesians fashion the hard wood into pegs to be used in carpentry and boat building.

Caesalpinia is named in honor of Andreas Caesalpini (1519–1603), Italian physician and botanist; *pulcherrima*, very beautiful, and *flava*, yellow, describe the flowers. Sometimes it is called dwarf poinciana because its flowers are similar to those of the royal poinciana *(Delonix regia)*. The Hawaiian name is 'ohai ali'i, or chief's poinciana, because of the red and yellow blossoms—colors that in older times were reserved for ruling chiefs.

HABIT	An erect, woody, partially deciduous shrub that grows to about 18 feet in height; has single or multiple, branching trunks, and a loose, open crown of delicate, fernlike, gray-green leaves. Frilly, butterfly-like, bright yellow flowers, each about 1½ inches, are borne in sparse clusters at tips of branches, the outer flowers blooming first. Flower clusters are produced nearly all year round; individual clusters bloom for several weeks. After flowering, many flat, woody, dark brown seedpods appear, each about 5 inches long. Fast growth rate; easily transplanted.
GROWING CONDITIONS	Quite adaptable; will grow in most places in Hawai'i; not a plant for the beach. Grows and blooms best in full sunny locations, planted in rich, well-watered, well-drained soil; defoliates readily in extremely dry or drought conditions.
USE	Specimen plant; mass planting; hedging; colorful flowers.
PROPAGATION	Easily grown from seeds.
INSECTS/DISEASES	Relatively insect free in Hawai'i.
PRUNING	May be pruned vigorously to induce new growth and flowering; January or February is the best time to prune the entire crown back to thick, woody branches.
FERTILIZING	Apply general garden fertilizer (10-30-10) to the planting bed at 4-month intervals.
DISADVANTAGES	Tends to become rangy in the winter months. Persistent, unsightly seedpods.

Calliandra emarginata
Powderpuff Plant, Tabardillo, Lehua Haole

This small, colorful Central American plant, known to Mexicans as tabardillo, was introduced to European horticulture in 1844 through a specimen plant collected near Acapulco. The Spanish word *tabardillo* means raging fever, or sunstroke; the name refers to the fiery red sunburst flowers which cover the plant during much of the year. In Hawai'i the powderpuff plant is sometimes called lehua haole, or foreign lehua (in reference to 'ōhi'a lehua, *Metrosideros collina* subsp. *polymorpha,* a native Hawaiian tree that bears similar sunburst flowers).

Powderpuff plant is used mainly as an ornamental. A close relative, *Calliandra anomala,* called cabeza de angel (angel's head) in Spanish has many uses in Central America. It is the source of an effective tanning agent; its flowers, crushed and mixed with water, are used in treating inflammation of the eye and ulcers of the skin; and juice from the leaves is specified for internal complaints.

Powderpuff plant is a small, delicate, specimen shrub. It has an interesting layered branching habit. As a container plant, it has few peers; its naturally dwarfed habit and delicate red flowers make it a fine bonsai plant.

Calliandra, from *kallos,* meaning beauty, and *andros,* meaning stamens, refers to the sunburst of stamens; *emarginata,* meaning having the margin removed, refers to the small notches at the tips of the leaves.

HABIT An erect, woody, evergreen shrub that grows to about 6 feet in height. The plant has a rather picturesque, crooked trunk and graceful tiers of horizontal branches. Has a loose, open crown of paired winglike leaflets. Tight, deep pink bud clusters burst into a puff composed of dozens of long, filamentous stamens; each puff is about 2 inches in diameter. Blossoms appear frequently throughout the year. Thin, narrow seedpods persist on the plant for long periods; when mature, the seedpods open explosively, twist back in a double curve, ejecting the seeds to some distance. Slow growth rate; easily transplanted.

GROWING CONDITIONS Fairly adaptable; will grow in many locations, from wet valleys to dry leeward slopes. It is not a beach plant, however. Prefers rich, well-watered, well-drained soils and wind-protected locations; blooms well either in full sun or partial shade.

USE Specimen plant; container plant; bonsai; colorful buds and flowers.

PROPAGATION Grown primarily from seeds or by cuttings.

INSECTS/DISEASES Relatively insect free.

PRUNING May be pruned judiciously to shape. The plant reacts well to restricted root growth and careful pruning involved in the techniques of bonsai culture.

FERTILIZING Apply general garden fertilizer (10-30-10) to the planting bed at 4-month intervals, and to container plants monthly. Water immediately and thoroughly.

DISADVANTAGES None.

Cassia alata
Candle Bush, Flor del Secreto, Akapulko

Candle bush is native to Central America, where it has been known and used since pre-Aztec times. It has been one of the most common and oldest known sources of American medicines. Probably its chief beneficial property is its effectiveness in the treatment of ringworm and other skin diseases. It is also thought to be effective in treating fevers and bites from insects and some kinds of poisonous snakes. A preparation from the seeds, taken internally, can be a remedy for intestinal worms; other parts of the plant produce a purgative. Although candle bush leaves are sometimes roasted and combined with another bean relative as a base for a coffee-like beverage, the plant is considered poisonous to livestock and fish. The bark yields tannin.

Candle bush has many descriptive ethnic names. The Aztecs knew it as ecapatli; today, Mexicans call it flor del secreto (secret flower), because of the hidden flowers nestled among the brilliant yellow bracts. People in the Philippines have named this imported plant akapulko, after the Mexican city (whose residents call the plant capulco). Its English name is most descriptive.

Cassia, from the Greek word, *kasia,* itself derived from an earlier Hebrew name for several related plants; *alata,* Latin for winged, describes the winglike ridges extending the length of the seedpods.

HABIT | An upright, woody, partially deciduous shrub that grows to about 10 feet in height and diameter; virtually trunkless, the plant produces numerous woody branches from the base upward. Large, heavy, glossy, bright green compound leaves grow to about 2 feet long; some of this foliage is lost during fall and early winter. Bright yellow, candle-like flower spikes, 8 to 10 inches long, bloom from late winter through summer. Long, woody, winged seedpods follow the blossoms. Fast growth rate (the plant will achieve full size within one year); easily transplanted if cut back to within one foot of the ground before being moved.

GROWING CONDITIONS | Very adaptable; will grow in most sunny garden locations, including beach areas with some protection; prefers hot, dry locations if constant ground moisture is available.

USE | Specimen plant; informal hedge; colorful flowers during winter and spring when many other plants are not in bloom.

PROPAGATION | By seeds or cuttings.

INSECTS/DISEASES | For scale, apply malathion or summer oil. For thrips, spray with diazinon or malathion. For grasshoppers, use one of the residual insecticides, such as carbaryl.

PRUNING | Should be cut back to about 1 foot from the ground in the fall, after seeds form; this procedure assures optimum bloom during the following season.

FERTILIZING | Apply general garden fertilizer (10-30-10) to the planting bed at 3-month intervals; water immediately and thoroughly. Fertilize heavily after annual pruning.

DISADVANTAGES | Plant becomes rangy if not drastically pruned.

Geraniaceae
(Geranium Family)

The name Geraniaceae comes from the Greek word *geranos,* meaning crane, which Dioscorides, the early naturalist, used to describe the long-beaked seed capsules of some geraniums. The family consists of five genera, *Geranium, Erodium, Monsonia, Pelargonium,* and *Sarcocaulon,* and about 750 species, most of them herbaceous in nature.

Most of the plants that gardeners refer to as geraniums are classified botanically as pelargoniums. These include the common **fish geranium (Pelargonium hortorum),** Martha Washington geranium *(P. domesticum),* ivy geranium *(P. peltatum),* and the aromatic rose geraniums *(P. graveolens).* Other than the pelargoniums, the family member probably most common in Hawaiian gardens is the tender groundcover heron's bill, or alfilaria *(Erodium circutarium).* Fourteen Hawaiian geraniums, nohu anu *(Geranium* spp.), grow wild at higher elevations on Hawai'i, Maui, and Kaua'i.

Pelargonium hortorum

Geranium, Fish Geranium, Stork's Bill, Laniuma, Kupukupu'ala

The common geraniums *(Pelargonium hortorum)* are actually horticultural hybrids that have been developed during the past 200 years from two South African parents, horseshoe geranium *(P. zonale)* and scarlet pelargonium *(P. inquinans)*. Sometimes these hybrids are collectively named fish geraniums, because of the faint fishlike odor that is released from the foliage. Some close relatives have practical uses: leaves and flowers of the rose geranium *(P. graveolens)* can be used as a substitute for attar of roses in soaps and perfumes; some cooks place a single leaf in the bottom of a glass in order to add flavor to mild-tasting jellies. Several other *Pelargonium* relatives are harvested for their essential oils, which are incorporated in perfumes.

Pelargonium, from *pelargos*, meaning stork, recalls the fruit's resemblance to a stork's bill (hence, one of its common names); *hortorum*, meaning belonging to the garden, relates to the hybrids' horticultural beginnings. Hawaiian names are laniuma, meaning curved sky, describing the shape of the flower cluster, and kupukupu'ala, meaning fragrant, spicy fern.

HABIT — An erect, bushy, evergreen shrub that grows to about 3 to 6 feet in height, depending on climate and horticultural variety. Irregular, sprawling, rather soft-stemmed branches are covered with soft, hairy, crinkly, highly scented leaves, 3 to 4 inches in diameter; leaf forms vary greatly with horticultural variety. Dense clusters of frilly flowers appear throughout the year, in colors that range from purple, red, and pink, to white. Pointed seedpods, about 1½ inches long, follow the blooms. Fast growth rate; easily transplanted, if plant is young. To transplant mature specimen, prune back drastically before moving.

GROWING CONDITIONS — Very adaptable, but will grow best in hot, dry, sunny locations if planted in rich, well-watered, well-drained soil.

USE — Specimen plant; mass planting; container plant; constant supply of colorful flowers.

PROPAGATION — Established varieties are propagated from cuttings, new varieties, from seed. Geranium cuttings are susceptible to stem-end rot; to control, dip cuttings in fungicide solution, such as captan, before applying growth regulator; use fungicide at rate of 1 tbsp. per gallon of water.

INSECTS/DISEASES — For moth caterpillar, apply one of the residual insecticides, such as carbaryl. Geraniums are especially subject to leaf spot; control by applying to foliage a fungicide, such as Dithane M-45, at the rate of 1 tbsp. per gallon of water.

PRUNING — Remove unsightly branches, dead leaves, and flower clusters.

FERTILIZING — Apply general garden fertilizer (10-30-10) to the planting bed at 3-month intervals, and to container plants at monthly intervals. Water immediately and thoroughly after each application. Overfertilization may cause the plant to produce excessive foliage and few flowers.

DISADVANTAGES — Highly subject to attack by moth caterpillars.

Rutaceae
(Rue Family)

The term Rutaceae is derived from the Greek word *rute,* which itself comes from *roumal,* meaning to preserve. People of olden times found that several members of this family had medicinal value, especially in promoting and preserving good health. The rues are a family of both temperate and tropical plants. While a few species are native to Asia and the Mediterranean region, most occur naturally in South Africa and Australia. The family includes 150 genera and about 900 species, most of which are shrubs or trees.

The most important genus in the rue family unquestionably is *Citrus.* This group of plants, native mainly to Asia, supplies the world with oranges *(Citrus sinensis),* grapefruit *(C. paradisi),* lemons *(C. limon),* limes *(C. aurantifolia),* mandarin oranges *(C. reticulata),* citrons *(C. medica),* calamondins *(Citrus* sp. × *Fortunella* sp. hybrid), and pummelos *(C. grandis).* Three other close relatives produce edible but less commonly used fruits: kumquat *(Fortunella japonica* and *F. margarita),* white sapote *(Casimiroa edulis),* and bael fruit *(Aegle marmelos).*

Native Hawaiian rues include mokihana *(Pelea anisata),* the island of Kaua'i's official plant, whose anise-scented fruits are strung into distinctive leis, and pilo-kea *(Platydesma* sp.), an attractive small tree. A relative not native to Hawai'i, but now one of the most important of the Islands' landscaping plants, is the mock orange *(Murraya paniculata),* the graceful South Pacific tree used most often in Hawai'i for hedges.

Atalantia buxifolia
Chinese Box-orange, Tsau Ping Lak, Severinia

The Chinese box-orange is native to southern China, Formosa, and Southeast Asia. The Cantonese know it as tsau ping lak (wine-cake thorn) because the berries are used in making leavened cakes. Many varieties of box-orange exist, usually identified by differing foliage forms. Chinese box-orange resists several diseases that attack other citrus species; it therefore makes a healthy rootstock for weaker, but desirably fruited, members of the genus. A close relative, *Atalantia monophylla,* from India, is important there in folk medicine: oil from the berries is applied externally for the relief of rheumatism and paralysis; a preparation from the root is considered to be an antiseptic and a stimulant; the leaves are used as an antidote for snakebite.

The box-orange is quite similar in appearance to the unrelated Japanese box *(Buxus microphylla* var. *japonica),* often seen in traditional gardens in Japan, and to the box *(B. sempervirens)* used throughout Europe and America in boxwood hedges.

Atalantia is named for Atalanta of Greek mythology, one of the Hesperides, the nymphs who guarded the garden where grew the golden apples that Gaea gave to Hera as a wedding gift; *buxifolia,* from *buxus,* meaning boxwood, and *folium,* meaning a leaf, describes the plant's foliage; severinia, once the accepted botanical name, still commonly used, is named for M. A. Severino (1580–1656), a lecturer on anatomy at Naples.

HABIT A low, spreading, evergreen shrub that grows to about 4 feet in height and diameter; has a dense, compact habit. Small, glossy, rounded, dark green leaves, about ½ inch in diameter, thickly cover the plant; new leaves are distinctively bronze. Clusters of small, white, fragrant citrus-like flowers appear toward the branch tips; flowers bloom at intervals throughout the year. Small, black ¼-inch berries follow the blossoms. Moderate growth rate; easily transplanted.

GROWING CONDITIONS The horticultural form commonly found in Hawai'i grows best in cool, moist, partially shaded or sunny locations. The plant will adapt to warmer, drier locations if it is allowed considerable and constant ground moisture.

USE Specimen plant; low hedge; container plant; bonsai plant; sometimes used as one of the rootstocks for citrus grafts.

PROPAGATION The horticultural forms are propagated from tip or woody stem cuttings. New kinds of ornamental stock are grown from seeds.

INSECTS/DISEASES For scale, spray with malathion or summer oil. For mealybugs, use diazinon or malathion.

PRUNING May be drastically pruned to shape; however, it generally needs little pruning.

FERTILIZING Apply general garden fertilizer (10-30-10) to the planting bed at 3-month intervals.

DISADVANTAGES Plant does have thorns, but these do not present a serious problem.

46

Euodia ridleyi
Evodia

The jungles of Southeast Asia have produced this colorful citrus relative. Evodia *(Euodia ridleyi)* is a purely ornamental plant. Several species of *Euodia* exist, however, that provide man with highly useful products. Some contain aromatic oils that act as coolants for fevers, as lotions for the improvement of complexions, and as tonics in the treatment of stomach complaints. A Javanese species, *E. latifolia,* contains a resin that, when dried, is mixed with coconut oil to make a varnish. Another Javanese species, *E. trichotoma,* has leaves that are considered to be vermicidal. A few species have wood suitable for lumber, either for house construction or for cabinetry.

Evodia is quite similar in appearance to the **Golden Prince panax.** The two plants, although frequently confused, are not related. Evodia, a native of tropical forests, is very much at home in partially shaded garden areas, where its yellow-green foliage forms a bright color accent. Evodia has a very upright growth habit, which allows it to be used in restricted planting areas, such as narrow side-yard spaces or small indoor containers.

Euodia, from the Greek *euodes,* meaning sweet-smelling, refers to the fragrant white flowers; *ridleyi* is named for Henry N. Ridley (1855–1956), Director of Gardens and Forests, Straits Settlements (1888–1912), and author of *Flora of the Malay Peninsula.* He introduced the para rubber tree *(Hevea brasiliensis),* chief source of natural rubber, to the Malay Peninsula.

HABIT An erect, woody, evergreen shrub that grows to about 4 feet in height. Dense, bushy, somewhat weeping crown composed of numerous pliant stems. Slender, glossy, three-parted, scalloped-edged leaves, 4 to 5 inches long, become bright yellow in full sun, darker green in shade. Inconspicuous white flowers are followed by small green to black fruits; flowers and fruits appear periodically throughout the year. Fast growth rate; easily transplanted.

GROWING CONDITIONS Adaptable, but not a good beach plant; requires constant moisture; grows best in rich, well-watered, well-drained soil.

USE Specimen plant; mass planting; unpruned hedge; container plant; colorful foliage.

PROPAGATION Usually by cuttings, but may be grown easily from seeds.

INSECTS/DISEASES For scale, apply malathion or summer oil.

PRUNING May be pruned vigorously to shape or to induce new growth; usually not pruned to severe formal shapes.

FERTILIZING Apply general garden fertilizer (10-30-10) to the planting bed at 3-month intervals, and to container plants at monthly intervals. Water immediately and thoroughly in each case. Plant may be susceptible to deficiencies in minor elements (evidenced by unhealthy, lackluster foliage); to correct this condition, apply fertilizers containing minor elements, either as foliar sprays or as additions to soil.

DISADVANTAGES May become rangy if not periodically pruned.

Triphasia trifolia
Limeberry, Limoncito, Limau Kelingket

As are many of its citrus relatives, limeberry is native to tropical Asia. It is found extensively both in the wild and under cultivation in Southeast Asia. Its Philippine name, limoncito (little lemon), and its Malaysian name, limau kelingket (sticky lime), aptly describe the tiny, dark, mucilaginous berries. Sometimes the fruits are preserved whole in syrup, the preparation being called Manila limeberries. They also are fermented to make a cordial, and are prepared as crystallized fruits. Malaysians and Filipinos ascribe medicinal and cosmetic qualities to the fruits: a medicine for treating chest diseases is made from the berries, and an aromatic bath salt is derived from the leaves. In Guam, the wood of the stem is used for making tool handles and charcoal.

Limeberry's small, glossy, dark green leaves give the plant a neat, well-ordered, attractive appearance. Its small structure and interesting natural branching system are highly regarded by bonsai trainers. In the garden, limeberries make excellent specimen plants, especially when set against large lava or coral boulders. They are often used in mass plantings or as low hedges.

Triphasia, meaning threefold, refers to the three-parted leaves; *trifolia,* meaning three leaves, also describes the species' foliar arrangement.

HABIT A spreading, woody, evergreen shrub that grows to about 10 feet in height. Single trunk with attractive lateral branches; dense crown of glossy, dark green leaves, each leaf about 1 inch across and composed of 3 equal-sized leaflets. Very thorny. Small, fragrant, white flowers are similar to those of other citrus species, but are smaller and bloom constantly throughout the year. Round, reddish purple, fleshy, mucilaginous fruits are about ½ inch in diameter; each contains several seeds; fruits have the distinct flavor and aroma of limes. Moderate growth rate; easily transplanted.

GROWING CONDITIONS Very adaptable; will grow almost anywhere except in extreme beach conditions. Prefers rich, well-watered, well-drained soil, full sun or partial shade.

USE Specimen plant; mass planting; container plant; bonsai.

PROPAGATION Almost always grown from seeds.

INSECTS/DISEASES For scale, apply malathion or summer oil. For thrips and mealybugs, use diazinon or malathion. For spider mites, spray with wettable sulfur. For citrus swallowtail butterfly caterpillars, apply one of the residual insecticides, such as carbaryl.

PRUNING Will withstand a great deal of pruning; may be shaped into severe, regimented forms. Pruning induces rapid new growth.

FERTILIZING Apply general garden fertilizer (10-30-10) to the planting bed at 3-month intervals, and to container plants at monthly intervals. Water immediately and thoroughly after each application. Sometimes exhibits brown-tipped or yellow foliage; this may indicate a lack of phosphorus, potash, or minor elements; apply 10-20-20 fertilizers with minor element additives to correct this condition. Water as above.

DISADVANTAGES Generally a trouble-free plant, but occasionally subject to insect infestation.

50

Malpighiaceae
(Malpighia Family)

The family Malpighiaceae is named for Marcello Malpighi (1628–1694), an Italian naturalist and professor at Bologna. It includes 60 genera and about 800 species, most of which are native to the tropics, especially those of South America. Shrubs and trees make up much of the family's membership, although immense climbing vines (lianas) are an impressive segment of the group.

Probably the family's most important commercial species is the acerola *(Malpighia punicifolia)*, the fruits of which are rich in vitamin C. Other relatives include nance *(Byrsonima crassifolia)*, an attractive small tree bearing edible fruits, and two well-known vines, climbing spray of gold *(Tristellateia australasiae)* and orchid vine *(Stigmaphyllon ciliatum)*.

Malpighia coccigera
Singapore Holly, Miniature Holly

This native of the Caribbean is commonly misnamed (as are many other plants), for it is not a holly nor is it a native of Singapore. As with so many misnomers of this sort, the plant was named by someone who did not know its history; because it was seen growing in Singapore, and looked like a holly, it received this descriptive appellation. In the tropics Singapore holly is used oftentimes as a substitute for true holly. The Chinese especially have adapted this plant to pot culture, training it on wood or wire frames into various topiary shapes.

In Hawai'i, Singapore holly is one of the most common plants found in borders and in rock gardens. Also, it is an excellent container plant, and takes well to pruning or bonsai culture. As an added attraction, Singapore holly produces handsome, lacy, pale pink flowers through much of the year. Orange berries appear along with the flowers.

The genus *Malpighia,* as well as the family, is named for Marcello Malpighi (1628–1694), Italian naturalist and professor at Bologna; *coccigera,* meaning berry-bearing, refers to the plant's constant fruiting habit.

HABIT | A vertical, woody, evergreen shrub that grows to about 6 feet in height. Single or multiple canelike trunks; the plant naturally has a loose crown, but gardeners almost always prune it into a dense, compact configuration. Small, holly-like leaves, about ½ inch in length, cluster along the branches. Dainty, pale pink flower clusters bloom constantly throughout the year. Red-orange, globular fruits, about ½ inch in diameter, follow the bloom. Slow growth rate; easily transplanted.

GROWING CONDITIONS | Very adaptable; will grow almost anywhere except in severe beach conditions; requires constant ground moisture.

USE | Specimen plant; mass planting; low hedge or border; container plant; bonsai; attractive flowers.

PROPAGATION | Almost always propagated from cuttings, but may be grown from seed.

INSECTS/DISEASES | For scale, spray with malathion or summer oil. For thrips and mealybugs, use diazinon or malathion.

PRUNING | May be pruned vigorously to shape and to induce new growth and flowering. Takes well either to structural shaping in bonsai culture or to close cropping employed in garden topiary work and hedging. Inclined to become bare-stemmed if pruning is done solely on the top; for fuller growth, prune plant at different stem heights.

FERTILIZING | Apply general garden fertilizer (10-30-10) to the planting bed at 2-month intervals, and to container plants at monthly intervals. Water immediately and thoroughly after each application. In sandy or poor soils, plant is susceptible to deficiencies in minor elements (evidenced by lackluster, yellowing foliage); to correct this condition, use fertilizers containing minor elements, either as foliar sprays or in soil applications.

DISADVANTAGES | None.

Thryallis glauca
Spray of Gold, Rama de Oro, Lluvia de Oro, Galphimia

Native to Central America and naturalized in the islands of the Caribbean, spray of gold is cultivated extensively throughout the tropical world. In Mexico the leaves are used to make a poultice for wounds, and a medicinal tea is brewed from the leaves "to purify the blood." The wood makes a fine kindling. Rama de oro is the Spanish version of the plant's English name, spray of gold; in Mexico and other parts of the Gulf and the Caribbean regions, the plant is known also as lluvia de oro (rain of gold).

If plants suffered from botanical identity-crises, spray of gold would be among the most bewildered ones. Early botanists first called it *Thryallis glauca.* Later the name was changed by Antonio José Cavanilles (1745–1804), a Spanish botanist and director of the botanical garden in Madrid, who somewhat whimsically dubbed it *Galphimia glauca,* devising the first of the binomials as an anagram of Malpighia. Recently, botanists have restored the original appellation. To complicate matters, spray of gold is constantly being confused with *Tristellateia australasiae,* climbing spray of gold, a look-alike and a relative to be sure, but a vine, not a shrub.

Spray of gold, with its bright yellow flowers, is one of Hawai'i's most colorful shrubs. Most often it serves as a specimen plant or as a constantly flowering low hedge.

Thryallis is an old Greek name for the plantain *(Plantago crassifolia),* an utterly unrelated plant; it is the generic name for several plants in the malpighia family; *glauca,* meaning silvery, refers to the velvety white "bloom" on stems and leaves.

HABIT
An erect, woody, evergreen shrub that grows to about 10 feet in height; loose crown composed of numerous sturdy branches. Small, oval, bright green leaves, about 1 inch long, cover the crown. Profuse, erect, bright yellow flower clusters are followed by many small orange berries. Fast growth rate; easily transplanted.

GROWING CONDITIONS
Very adaptable; prefers full sun, rich soil, constant ground moisture.

USE
Specimen plant; mass planting; untrimmed hedge; colorful flowers.

PROPAGATION
Usually propagated from cuttings but may be started from seed.

INSECTS/DISEASES
For scale, apply malathion or summer oil. For thrips, use diazinon or malathion.

PRUNING
May be pruned vigorously to induce new growth and flowering. Not a good material for severely tailored hedges because such trimming eliminates most of the flowering tips.

FERTILIZING
Apply general garden fertilizer (10-30-10) to the planting bed at 3-month intervals. Water immediately and thoroughly after each application.

DISADVANTAGES
May become quite rangy without occasional pruning.

Euphorbiaceae
(Spurge Family)

The Euphorbiaceae, one of the plant kingdom's larger families includes about 300 genera and 5,000 species. The family is widespread, having representatives that are native to most of the growing regions of the world. Many spurges are of considerable economic importance, producing such diverse materials as medicines, poisons, dyes, rubber, fibers, oils, starches, resins, edible fruits, and wood. In addition, many spurges are extremely ornamental.

Important economic spurges include castor bean *(Ricinus communis)*, from which castor oil is expressed, Ceará rubber *(Manihot glaziovii)*, whose latex is one source of natural rubber, and physic nut *(Jatropha curcas)*, whose sap is used both as a fish poison and as a medicinal poultice. The most prominent euphorbia associated with Hawai'i is an import from the tropical Pacific. It is the kukui *(Aleurites moluccana)*, which was brought to Hawai'i by early Polynesian migrants as a source of oil, dyes, food condiments, medicines, and light.

Euphorbia is the Latin name for spurges. The name was given to these plants by Dioscorides, a Greek naturalist of the second century A.D., in honor of Euphorbus, physician to King Juba of Mauritania (part of present-day Algeria). Juba was the husband of Selene, daughter of Cleopatra and Mark Antony. Dioscorides compiled *De Materia Medica,* the Western world's most important pharmacological text before the eighteenth century.

Acalypha godseffiana var. *heterophylla*
Acalypha, Three-Seeded Mercury

Acalyphas were named indirectly by Hippocrates. The Greek physician (ca. 460–370 B.C.), known as the "father of medicine," gave the name *acalephe* to a nettle he described. Latter-day botanists transferred the latinized word to this group of plants in the spurge family. Acalyphas as a group generally are called beefsteak plant, copper leaf, or three-seeded Mercury.

Acalypha godseffiana, a species from New Guinea, has large, oval, flat, green and white leaves. Its variety *heterophylla* often is mistaken for one of the panaxes because its long, thin, irregular, shaggy foliage is somewhat similar to that of the feathery panax varieties. This plant is often seen as hedging in Hawai'i, particularly along the roadsides and in the small towns on the island of Kaua'i. Acalypha is an excellent privacy plant; grows tall and dense providing both visual screening and protection from the wind. Recently a colored, dwarfed, form of the plant, similar in its long, irregular leaf structure, but distinctly rose-red in cast, has been introduced into Hawai'i.

Acalypha, from *acalephe,* meaning a stinging nettle, refers to the plant's irritating sap; *godseffiana* is named in honor of Joseph Godseff (ca. 1846–1921), a plant collector for the English nursery trade; *heterophylla,* from *heteros,* meaning different, and *phylla,* meaning leaves, refers to the extremely irregular, shaggy, wide to narrow leaves exhibited on each plant.

HABIT
A vertical, somewhat weeping, woody, evergreen shrub that grows to about 15 feet in height and has a dense crown with numerous arching branches. Narrow, irregular, variegated green and yellow leaves densely cover the plant in a weeping manner. The flowers are insignificant. Not known to fruit in Hawai'i. Moderately fast growth rate; easily transplanted, but cuttings root so readily that plants seldom are moved.

GROWING CONDITIONS
Adaptable. Prefers cool, moist areas and full sun, but will grow in drier locations if the root mass is kept constantly moist. Not a beach plant.

USE
Specimen plant; container plant; colorful foliage; tropical effect; almost always used as a hedge.

PROPAGATION
Grows easily from cuttings.

INSECTS/DISEASES
For Chinese rose beetles, apply one of the residual insecticides, such as carbaryl. For thrips, use diazinon or malathion. For spider mites, apply wettable sulfur. For scale, spray with malathion or summer oil.

PRUNING
May be pruned to almost any size. Prune drastically to encourage new growth, vigorous foliage, a dense crown.

FERTILIZING
Apply general garden fertilizer (10-30-10) to the planting bed at 4-month intervals, and to container plants at monthly intervals. Water immediately and thoroughly after each application. In sandy or poor soils, plant is susceptible to deficiencies of minor elements (evidenced by yellowing foliage); to correct this condition, use fertilizers containing minor elements, either as foliar sprays or as soil additions.

DISADVANTAGES
Very susceptible to Chinese rose beetles and other pests.

Acalypha hamiltoniana
Acalypha, Picotee Acalypha

This acalypha was found growing in an English nursery in 1895, probably a result of natural cross-pollination of other acalyphas growing there. Its leaves are faintly reminiscent of fans, highly convoluted and seeming to have been trimmed by nature's pinking shears. The creamy white borders of the leaves appear to have been painted by hand. This acalypha's most common form produces green and white leaves; less common is a form whose green and white leaves are tinted with pink. At times both color forms may exhibit oval, perfectly flat, unpleated leaves, which probably represent a reversion to characteristics of one or both of the unknown parents.

In Hawai'i, *Acalypha hamiltoniana* is most commonly used as a large dense hedge. Its exotic foliage produces a decidedly tropical effect and forms an excellent background for other dramatic foliage plants. Unfortunately, like other acalyphas, it is highly susceptible to attack by Chinese rose beetles, especially in the warmer lowland regions of the Islands. Beetle damage is much less severe in higher areas with cooler climate and greater rainfall.

Acalypha, from *acalephe,* a name first applied to a nettle, refers to the plant's sometimes irritating sap; *hamiltoniana* is named for Francis Buchanan-Hamilton (1762–1829), a British botanist and superintendent of the botanic garden at Calcutta.

HABIT
A vertical, woody, evergreen shrub that grows to about 15 feet in height and forms a dense crown composed of numerous erect branches. Large curly leaves have unusual undulating, serrated edges; leaves generally green with white margins, although one form has those colors overcast with pink. Flowers appear in insignificant pendent clusters. Not known to fruit in Hawai'i. Moderately fast growth rate; easily transplanted, but cuttings are so readily rooted that older plants are seldom moved.

GROWING CONDITIONS
Very adaptable. Prefers cool, moist areas and full sun, but will grow in drier locations if the root mass is kept constantly moist.

USE
Specimen plant; container plant; colorful foliage; almost always used as a hedge.

PROPAGATION
Grows easily from cuttings.

INSECTS/DISEASES
For Chinese rose beetles, apply one of the residual insecticides, such as carbaryl. For thrips, use diazinon or malathion. For spider mites, apply wettable sulfur. For scale, spray with malathion or summer oil.

PRUNING
May be pruned to almost any size; prune drastically to encourage new growth, vigorous foliage, a dense crown.

FERTILIZING
Apply general garden fertilizer (10-30-10) to the planting bed at 4-month intervals and to container plants at monthly intervals. Water immediately and thoroughly after each application. In sandy or poor soils plant is susceptible to deficiencies in minor elements (evidenced by yellowing foliage); to correct this condition, apply fertilizers containing minor elements, either as foliar sprays or as additions to soil.

DISADVANTAGES
Very susceptible to Chinese rose beetles and other pests.

Acalypha hispida
Chenille Plant, Red-hot Cat's Tail

This native of New Guinea and Indonesia produces flower clusters that show a striking resemblance to the familiar chenille of weaving. Some people see in such a flower a red-hot cat's tail. Indonesians sometimes eat the boiled young leaves as a vegetable, although the cooking process requires several changes of water in order to remove the natural irritants present in the foliage. An infusion of the roots, bark, leaves, and flowers is used medicinally as a worming agent, as a remedy for colic and intestinal disorders, and as a poultice for sores. In India the leaves are beaten with green tobacco root and a rice preparation for treatment of certain cutaneous ulcers.

Acalypha hispida is the most common of the chenille plants. Two varieties are also used in landscaping; the horticultural variety *alba* has white flower clusters, while the variety *ramosa* produces multiple red flower clusters. This latter variety is sometimes called Philippine Medusa because its skeins of flowers suggest the snaky-locked Gorgon of Greek mythology. In southwestern United States, potted chenilles often are used as Christmas plants.

Acalypha, from *acalephe,* meaning a stinging nettle, refers to the plant's irritating sap; *hispida,* meaning rough and shaggy, refers to the plant's hairy stems, leaves, and flowers; *alba* means white; *ramosa,* meaning branching, refers to that variety's multiple-branching flower habit.

HABIT
An upright, woody, evergreen shrub that grows to about 12 feet in height; has a full crown composed of numerous erect branches, covered by large, handsome, spade-shaped, dark green leaves. Foot-long, pendent, red chenille-like flower clusters bloom at intervals throughout much of the year. Not known to fruit in Hawai'i. Moderately fast growth rate; easily transplanted.

GROWING CONDITIONS
Prefers cool, moist areas and full sun, but will grow in drier locations if the root mass is kept constantly moist.

USE
Specimen plant; container plant; hedge; colorful tropical flowers.

PROPAGATION
Grows easily from cuttings.

INSECTS/DISEASES
For Chinese rose beetles, apply one of the residual insecticides, such as carbaryl. For thrips, use diazinon or malathion. For spider mites, apply wettable sulfur. For scale, spray with malathion or summer oil.

PRUNING
After peak flowering periods, plant should be pruned back to the woody branches to induce new growth. Periodic pruning will promote maximum flowering.

FERTILIZING
Apply general garden fertilizer (10-30-10) to the planting bed at 4-month intervals, to container plants monthly; water immediately and thoroughly. In sandy or poor soils, plant is susceptible to deficiencies in minor elements (evidenced by yellowing foliage); apply fertilizers containing minor elements to correct this condition.

DISADVANTAGES
Very susceptible to Chinese rose beetles and other pests.

Acalypha wilkesiana
Beefsteak Plant, Jacob's Coat, Copper Leaf

The red beefsteak plant is native to Fiji and the New Hebrides. Many other kinds of ''beefsteaks'' are indigenous to the Pacific tropics, and several are used throughout the Malaysian-Indonesian archipelago as medicines and herbs. As with its cousin the chenille plant, the beefsteak plant's leaves are sometimes eaten as a vegetable, although several boilings and changes of water are necessary in order to remove the natural irritants present in the foliage. Beefsteak plants are included in lists of emergency foods recommended in jungle survival courses taught to American military personnel.

The beefsteak plant is so called because its leaves resemble thin slices of raw beef. Other names given the plant are Jacob's coat (because the leaves appear in many color combinations), copper leaf, and match-me-if-you-can (alluding to the impossibility of finding two leaves with identical markings).

Acalypha, from *acalephe,* meaning a stinging nettle, refers to the plant's irritating sap; *wilkesiana* is named for Lieutenant Charles Wilkes, U.S.N. (1798–1877), commander of the U.S. Exploring Expedition to the Pacific, 1838–1842.

HABIT An erect, woody, evergreen shrub that grows to about 15 feet in height. The full crown is composed of numerous erect branches. Large, curly, serrated, mottled leaves, 5 to 6 inches in diameter; leaf colors vary from green to yellow to pink to red. Insignificant flowers bloom at intervals throughout the year on the new growth. Not known to produce fruit in Hawai'i. Moderately fast growth rate; easily transplanted, but cuttings are so easily rooted that older plants are seldom moved.

GROWING CONDITIONS Very adaptable; prefers cool, moist areas and full sun, but will grow in drier locations if the root mass is kept constantly moist.

USE Specimen plant; container plant; colorful tropical foliage; usually used as a hedge.

PROPAGATION Easily grown from cuttings.

INSECTS/DISEASES For Chinese rose beetles, apply one of the residual insecticides, such as carbaryl. For thrips, use diazinon or malathion. For spider mites, apply wettable sulfur. For scale, spray with malathion or summer oil.

PRUNING May be pruned to almost any size; prune drastically to encourage new growth, vigorous foliage, a dense crown.

FERTILIZING Apply general garden fertilizer (10-30-10) to the planting bed at 4-month intervals, and to container plants at monthly intervals. Water immediately and thoroughly after each application. In sandy or poor soils, plant is susceptible to deficiencies in minor elements (evidenced by yellowing foliage); apply fertilizers containing minor elements, either as foliar sprays or as additions to soil, to correct this condition.

DISADVANTAGES Very susceptible to Chinese rose beetles and other insect pests.

Breynia nivosa var. *rosi-picta*
Snow Bush, Sweet Pea Bush, Hujan Panas

One of Hawai'i's many plants with variegated foliage is the snow bush, a native of the South Pacific islands. Although snow bush has little value other than its use as an ornamental, other *Breynia* species have bark that both Filipinos and Mexicans process into an astrigent medicine for the treatment of hemorrhage. In Bihar State, India, a *Breynia*'s leaves are smoked like tobacco for the treatment of tonsillitis. In Malaysia, leaves of a native species are used for making poultices. Malaysians call the plants hujan panas, meaning red rain, because the small red fruits give the illusion of hot red raindrops falling from the branches.

Color variation in the foliage is determined by the amount of sunlight the plant receives. Foliage that grows deep green in the shade will turn pink and white in bright sunlight. Oftentimes from afar, the bright-leaved plant appears to have many pink and white blossoms covering its entire surface. *B. nivosa,* the parent species, produces green and white foliage; its variety *rosi-picta,* most commonly seen in Hawaiian gardens, has green, white, and pink foliage. Another variety, *atropurpurea,* has dark green and purple foliage.

Breynia is named in honor of Johann Philipp Breyn (1637–1716), a noted German botanist and author of *Prodromi Fasciculi Rariorum Plantarum; nivosa,* snowy, describes the frilly white leaves; *rosi-picta,* means rose-painted.

HABIT A spreading, somewhat weeping evergreen shrub that grows to about 12 feet in height; multiple stems form a loose billowing crown. Small colorful leaves about ¾ inch in length; younger foliage delicately white and pink giving the shrub a snow-covered appearance; older foliage mostly green. Insignificant flowers and fruits appear at intervals throughout the year. A single plant produces numerous offshoots from underground stems. Fast growth rate; easily transplanted.

GROWING CONDITIONS Very adaptable, even to beach conditions if protected from heavy salt winds; prefers rich soil, constant ground moisture; grows either in full sun or in partial shade but is much more colorful in strong sunlight.

USE Specimen plant; mass planting; informal hedge; container plant; colorful foliage.

PROPAGATION Larger plants may be established by separating root offshoots from base of parent plant, or may be propagated from cuttings.

INSECTS/DISEASES For Chinese rose beetles, apply one of the residual insecticides, such as carbaryl. For scale, use malathion or summer oil.

PRUNING May be vigorously pruned to induce new, colorful growth. Pruning also limits plant size and area of spread.

FERTILIZING Apply general garden fertilizer (10-30-10) to the planting bed at 3-month intervals, and to container plants at monthly intervals. Water immediately and thoroughly after each application.

DISADVANTAGES Plant has an aggressive root system which sends up numerous offshoots in areas where they are not wanted.

Codiaeum variegatum
Croton

This plant of many foliar colors and shapes is native to the western South Pacific. Crotons are extremely useful to Southeast Asians: the leaves provide a nourishing fodder for animals, and the roots and leaves afford people poultices for treating sores. When young, certain yellow-leaved varieties are used in Malaysia as a food flavoring; older leaves, containing irritants, will burn the mouth. In Melanesia, where different villages select local varieties as emblems, crotons play a part in rites and ceremonies; the leaves are often used as ornaments for the hair. In India the powdered leaves are applied externally in treatment of certain abdominal-digestive complaints.

Variation is the descriptive catchword for this kaleidoscopic plant. Literally hundreds of different foliage forms and color patterns exist in the wild; new varieties constantly develop from natural cross-pollination among foliar forms. Horticulturists, too, during the last hundred years, have propagated many new forms by selective hybridization. Many varieties have been given descriptive names, such as cup-and-saucer, corkscrew, Indian blanket, oak leaf, duck's foot (shown here), sampan, and ram's horn.

Codiaeum probably is derived from the Malayan names for the plant, kodiho and codebo; *variegatum,* meaning variegated, refers to the leaf colors. *Kroton* means tick in Greek; its Latin derivative, *croton,* is the accepted botanical name for a separate plant group in the **bean family (Leguminosae).** So, botanically speaking, the plants we call crotons are not *Crotons* at all.

HABIT A large, almost treelike, evergreen shrub that grows to about 25 feet in height; usually pruned to a dense, shrubby form 4 to 8 feet high; woody trunk and branches support a thick, dense crown; overall shape and size differ somewhat with the variety. Glossy, multicolored leaves are produced in many sizes and shapes according to the variety. Insignificant flower clusters bloom at intervals throughout the year. Small fruits follow the blossoms. New varieties develop from seeds. Moderate growth rate; easily transplanted.

GROWING CONDITIONS Very adaptable; grows well in almost any sunny location, even at the beach if protected from heavy salt winds; the bright, colorful foliage is best produced in bright sunlight; needs constant, considerable ground moisture for best foliar growth.

USE Specimen plant; container plant; mass planting; hedge; small tree; grown primarily for colorful foliage.

PROPAGATION Airlayer branches to propagate large specimens. Cuttings taken from branch tips or woody stems will root readily. May be propagated by seeds.

INSECTS/DISEASES For scale, apply malathion or summer oil. For thrips and mealybugs, use diazinon or malathion. For spider mites, spray with wettable sulfur.

FERTILIZING Apply general garden fertilizer (10-30-10) to the planting bed at 2-month intervals, and to container plants monthly. Water immediately and thoroughly.

DISADVANTAGES Sap can irritate skin and stain clothing.

Euphorbia cotinifolia
Hierba Mala

Hierba mala (weed) is the vernacular name for this tropical American plant. Central Americans consider it to be both good and bad, having used it both to cure and to kill. Its milky sap, highly poisonous and irritating to internal organs, eyes, and skin, has been used medicinally for centuries as a drastic emetic and cathartic. Fishermen spread the sap over their fishing grounds to stun their prey, which rise to the surface incapacitated. Poison for arrowheads and other lethal preparations have been made from the plant by the natives of Curaçao. The Earl of Portland introduced this interesting plant into England in 1690.

Unlike its close relative **poinsettia (Euphorbia pulcherrima)**, which produces its colorful leaves (usually considered flowers) only during the winter months, hierba mala provides colorful foliage the year round. The attractive shrub may either be trained into a small tree or shaped by clipping into a dense bush. Generally it is shown as an interesting garden specimen; sometimes, however, large hedges and other mass arrangements are seen. Hierba mala's poisonous qualities should not preclude its use in landscaping; if treated with respect, it is no more harmful than many other common garden plants.

Euphorbia was named for the second-century A.D. Mauritanian physician, Euphorbus; *cotinifolia* is from *Rhus cotinus,* the smoke tree, and *folium,* meaning a leaf; the whole name, then, means ''the *Euphorbia* with leaves like those of *Rhus cotinus.''*

HABIT An erect, woody, evergreen shrub that grows to about 20 feet in height in an upward-branching, round-headed, billowing form. It is purely a foliage plant, with a distinctive bronze-red-violet color, both in branches and in leaves. Insignificant flowers and fruit add little to its appearance; each seedpod contains three seeds. Moderate growth rate; easily transplanted.

GROWING CONDITIONS Very adaptable; grows nearly everywhere in Hawai'i except in extreme salt conditions; thrives in hot, dry, sunny areas if adequate and constant ground moisture is supplied. To produce its most vivid foliage, the plant must have full sun.

USE Specimen plant; mass planting; container plant; colorful foliage.

PROPAGATION Generally propagated by cuttings.

INSECTS/DISEASES None of any consequence.

PRUNING Withstands drastic pruning. May be cut back severely and periodically to shape and to induce new, colorful foliage. Requires little pruning, however, and may be allowed to grow naturally into a large rounded mass.

FERTILIZING Apply general garden fertilizer (10-30-10) to the planting bed at 2-month intervals, to container plants monthly. Water immediately and thoroughly each time.

DISADVANTAGES The sap is highly poisonous and irritating, especially to people who are allergic or sensitive to other substances.

Euphorbia leucocephala

Flor de Niño, Little Child's Flower, Little Boy Flower, Christ Child's Flower

This is the little child's flower, or more usually, the Christ Child's flower, of Central America. Like its close relative **poinsettia *(Euphorbia pulcherrima)*,** flor de niño is a short-day plant, blooming only during the months when the least amount of sunlight reaches the earth. In the Southern Hemisphere it blooms in July and August. As it blooms during the Christmas season in the Northern Hemisphere, the Christian faithful have considered its immaculate purity as symbolic of the Christ Child.

Flor de niño, like other euphorbias, has a poisonous milky sap; little mention has been made of any curative uses.

During much of the year the plant is visually recessive, hiding in the garden under a canopy of unobtrusive gray-green foliage. As the days grow short, however, a metamorphosis sets in: the ugly duckling becomes a lovely swan. As the flowers begin to bloom, the small leaf clusters surrounding the flower spikes turn from green to a perfect white. When the days lengthen, the white bracts fall from the plant and once again the gray-green leaves appear.

Euphorbia was named for the second-century A.D. Mauritanian physician Euphorbus; *leucocephala,* from *leucus,* meaning white, and *cephalaeus,* meaning belonging to the head, refers to the plant's winter crown of white.

HABIT An erect, woody, nearly evergreen plant that grows to about 20 feet in height, and is gracefully upright, with a rounded, open crown. In early winter, the plant turns from gray-green to white, as flower bracts form a dense mantle over the entire crown. After flowering, the plant loses much of its foliage for a very short time; then new leaves appear. Tiny flowers and seeds are of little importance visually; each seedpod contains three seeds. Fast growth rate; easily transplanted.

GROWING CONDITIONS Very adaptable; will grow almost anywhere in Hawai'i except in extreme salt conditions. For best winter coloration, must be grown in a very sunny location but away from artificial night lighting, which prevents optimum flowering. Constant ground moisture is required for healthy growth.

USE Specimen plant; mass planting; container plant; colorful bracts.

PROPAGATION By seeds or cuttings.

INSECTS/DISEASES None of any consequence.

PRUNING Withstands drastic pruning; may be pruned back to any desired height. Best color occurs if plant is heavily pruned in late winter, directly after the year's flowering.

FERTILIZING Apply general garden fertilizer (10-30-10) to the planting bed at 2-month intervals, and to container plants at monthly intervals. Water immediately and thoroughly after each application.

DISADVANTAGES None of any consequence.

Euphorbia pulcherrima
Poinsettia, Flor de Pascua, Flor de Noche Buena

The poinsettia is native to Mexico, where it is called flor de Pascua (flower of Christmas) or flor de noche buena (Christmas Eve flower). The plant has been highly useful since pre-Aztec times. Its sap, caustic to the eye, irritating to the skin, and poisonous when taken internally, is used sometimes as a depilatory. Leaves are applied as a poultice in the treatment of erysipelas and similar cutaneous infections. In Central America the red bracts and smaller white flowers sometimes are made into a liquid taken internally by nursing mothers, in exceedingly dangerous attempts to increase their flow of milk. Aztecs processed the bark and bracts to make an important red dye.

Like the chrysanthemum, the poinsettia is a short-day plant. In the Northern Hemisphere, poinsettias are at their height of bloom at Christmastime, and therefore have become one of the most popular yuletide plants. Indeed, Filipinos call the plant Pascua (Christmas).

Euphorbia was named for the second-century A.D. Mauritanian physician Euphorbus; *pulcherrima,* meaning beautiful, refers to the brilliant red floral bracts. The name poinsettia honors Joel Roberts Poinsett (1779–1851), American minister to Mexico from 1825 to 1829, who sent the first seeds of this plant to the United States (to Charleston, South Carolina) in 1828.

HABIT	A sprawling, woody, evergreen shrub that grows to about 18 feet in height. Light green, velvety leaves, 6 to 8 inches long, on irregular arching branches. Insignificant green and yellow flowers are surrounded by spectacular white, pink, or red floral leaves. Bears tiny, 3-seeded pods. Rapid growth rate; easily transplanted.
GROWING CONDITIONS	Very adaptable; will grow almost anywhere with constant ground moisture; exposure to salt winds or spray will damage plants. Show best color in sunny areas.
USE	Specimen plant; mass planting; container plant; colorful flowers in winter.
PROPAGATION	Named varieties are propagated from woody cuttings, new varieties from seed.
INSECTS/DISEASES	For scale, apply malathion or summer oil. For thrips and mealybugs, use diazinon or malathion. For spider mites, spray with wettable sulfur.
PRUNING	In Hawai'i, prune severely in early February and again in early August; plant will begin to bloom in November, when days grow short.
FERTILIZING	Apply general garden fertilizer (10-30-10) to the planting bed at 2-month intervals, and to container plants at monthly intervals. Plant is susceptible to deficiencies in minor elements (evidenced by browning of leaf edges and deformed foliage); to correct this condition, apply fertilizers containing minor elements.
DISADVANTAGES	Because artificial illumination interferes with normal flowering, lights from streets and from residences can inhibit blooming. Container plants grown for interior decoration often are overwatered or underwatered, may be attacked by spider mites, or receive too much shade or draft. Foliage and flowers will fall as a result.

Manihot esculenta

Variegated Cassava, Tapioca, Manioka

Because its roots are rich in starch, cassava, a native of Brazil, is one of the world's important food crops, especially for the peoples of Africa, tropical America, and some Pacific islands. Generally the root is cooked and eaten in much the same way as is the Irish potato. The variegated form of *M. esculenta* is primarily an ornamental shrub.

There are many cultivars of cassava; generally, these varieties are either the sweet types, from which are made flour (called *farinha de mendioca*) and tapioca, or the bitter varieties, which are eaten as vegetables after several changes of water in which they are cooked. Bitter cassava is used also in the production of cassareep, a powerful antiseptic that is also an ingredient in Worcestershire-type sauces. In some countries cassava root is made into sizings for fabrics and mucilage for postage stamps. Brazilians use extracts from cassava plants to preserve meat and to stupefy fish they wish to catch. The roots of some cassavas are made into livestock feed in the United States.

In tropical West Africa a decoction of cassava bark is considered to be an antirheumatic agent, and the powdered leaves are applied to the head in a compress for treating fever and headaches. In Cambodia and India the cut root, considered to be antiseptic, is applied to wounds.

Manihot is an old Brazilian Indian name for the plant; *esculenta*, meaning good to eat, refers to the starch-laden root.

HABIT An erect, woody, evergreen shrub that grows to about 8 feet in height. As the plant matures, lower stems, characterized by knobby, swollen nodes, become completely bare. The thick upper crown is covered with large, deeply-lobed leaves about 6 inches in diameter; the foliage is mostly white, with irregular green edging and bright red veins and leaf stems. Tiny flowers are followed by round, ½-inch seedpods. Rapid growth rate (cuttings mature in one year); easily transplanted.

GROWING CONDITIONS Very adaptable, will grow nearly everywhere, although it is not a good beach plant; it grows best in areas of rich, well-watered, well-drained soil, in full sun.

USE Specimen plant; mass planting; hedging; container plant; colorful foliage.

PROPAGATION This plant must be propagated from stem cuttings to preserve variegated foliage. Seeds sprout easily, but generally produce green-foliaged plants. Most tapiocas are propagated from cuttings because full plant growth is achieved much more quickly. Plant 12-inch woody cuttings upright, in place, in the garden.

INSECTS/DISEASES For scale, spray with malathion or summer oil.

PRUNING May be pruned vigorously to shape and to contain growth; can be cut back drastically to ground level, yet will grow back quickly.

FERTILIZING Apply general garden fertilizer (10-30-10) to the planting bed at 3-month intervals and to container plants at monthly intervals. Water immediately and thoroughly.

DISADVANTAGES Relatively short-lived; the plants tend to deteriorate after a few years.

Aquifoliaceae
(Holly Family)

The family Aquifoliaceae takes its name from one of its members, *Ilex aquifolium*. The specific name, in turn, is derived from *aqui*, meaning point, and *folium*, meaning leaf, and describes the hollies' familiar needle-pointed leaves. The holly family is subdivided into two genera, the lesser-known *Nemopanthus*, and the widely known *Ilex*. About 400 species of hollies are recognized, most of which can be classified as tropical or temperate-zone trees and shrubs. Hollies are dioecious; that is, separate male and female plants exist, the pollen from the flower of the male plant being needed to fertilize the ovules of the female plant.

The best-known member, probably, is the English holly *(Ilex aquifolium)*, the celebrated holly of Christmas tradition and decoration. Chinese holly *(I. cornuta)*, dahoon *(I. cassine)*, and yerba maté *(I. paraguariensis)* are other common ornamental species. A native of Hawai'i is kāwa'u *(I. anomala)*. Mountain holly *(Nemopanthus mucronatus)*, a handsome, shrubby bush, is native to North America.

Ilex dimorphophylla
Okinawan Holly

Okinawan holly is one of about 400 species of holly found growing in the temperate and tropical regions of the world. This species is native to Amamiōshima, one of the Ryūkyū Islands of southern Japan. Okinawan holly is closely related to the Japanese holly or inu-tsuge *(Ilex crenata),* a common hedge plant and clipped shrub in Japanese gardens. Another relative is mochi-no-ki *(I. integra),* which is used by Japanese in the production of birdlime, a sticky substance made from pounded holly bark that is employed to capture small birds and insects. Another species, soyogo *(I. pedunculosa),* has leaves that are boiled to make a brown dye. Soyogo is seldom seen in Japanese gardens; however, inu-tsuge and mochi-no-ki are often used ornamentally as topiary plants in traditional gardens and as bonsai.

Recently, Okinawan holly has been imported into northern Japan and Hawai'i. Gardeners have taken immediate interest in the plant because of its small, delicate branches and foliage, which is crisply clean, tidy, and handsome. It is an ideal container plant, suitable for natural pruning or bonsai training. It is a lover of sunny spots and grows happily in open rock gardens, unshaded terraces, and lanais.

Ilex is the ancient name for one of the European oaks, *Quercus ilex;* plants in the genus *Ilex* may have been so named because of the similarity between the wavy, serrated edges of oak leaves and holly leaves; *dimorphophylla,* from *di,* meaning two, *morpho,* meaning form or shape, and *phylla,* meaning leaf, refers to the plant's varied leaf forms.

HABIT	An erect, woody, evergreen shrub that grows to about 5 feet in height in Hawai'i; has a naturally dense, formal cone shape; branches grow closely together. The crown is composed of many small, ½-inch-long, prickly or smooth-edged leaves. Small white flowers are followed by bright red berries in winter and early spring. Slow growth rate; easily transplanted.
GROWING CONDITIONS	Adaptable; will grow in most areas, even at the beach if protected from extreme salt conditions. Grows best in full sun and warm locations; it becomes loose-limbed and attenuated if kept in the shade, but will grow well indoors if placed near a sunlit door or window. Requires constant ground moisture, and rich, well-drained soil.
USE	Specimen plant; mass planting; low-trimmed hedge; container plant; bonsai.
PROPAGATION	Grown from cuttings.
INSECTS/DISEASES	None known in Hawai'i.
PRUNING	Requires little or no pruning if natural shape is desired; can be heavily pruned to shape for hedging, topiary, or bonsai cultivation.
FERTILIZING	Apply general garden fertilizer (10-30-20) to the planting bed at 3-month intervals, and to container plants monthly. Water immediately and thoroughly each time.
DISADVANTAGES	None.

Leeaceae
(Leea Family)

The family Leeaceae is named for its only genus, *Leea*. Originally classified as members of the grape family (Vitidaceae), the leeas now are considered to be separate from those convivial calabash cousins. About 70 species of *Leea* are recognized.

Two species are grown in Hawai'i; one, the shrub **Leea coccinea,** is described in this book. The others, *L. manillensis* and *L. sambucina,* are very similar plants. Although several *Leea* species are cultivated throughout the world, most are relatively unknown to ornamental horticulture.

Leea coccinea
Amamali

Leea coccinea, Burmese in origin, is one of about 70 members of the Leeaceae found growing throughout tropical Africa, Asia, and the Pacific islands. Leeas are sometimes called treebines (tree vines) because many of the species begin as scrambling shrubs but eventually climb 40 or more feet in height, becoming twining trees in the process. Amamali and mali-mali are Filipino names that are widely used for several of the leeas. Two other species, one *(L. manillensis)* from the Philippines and another *(L. sambucina)* from India and Malaysia, also are grown ornamentally in Hawai'i. *L. aquata,* of Indonesia, has wood that is grated with ginger root *(Zingiber officinale)* and leaves of the **caricature plant *(Graptophyllum pictum),*** to compound a medicine used in the treatment of paralysis. Other Southeast Asian species are employed variously in the treatment of headache, colic, ringworm, tapeworm, ulcers of the skin, and falling hair.

The amamalis resemble certain panax species (see ***Polyscias* spp.).** They are upright, dark green shrubs, densely foliaged. They are excellent container plants, highly useful either inside or outside the house. This particular species, unlike many of its relatives, has brilliant clusters of red buds that give way to handsome pink flowers and clusters of purple fruits. Blossoms and fruits begin to appear on the plant when it is quite young.

The genus *Leea* is named in honor of James Lee (1715–1795), a London nurseryman; *coccinea,* meaning scarlet, describes the red buds.

HABIT An erect, woody, evergreen shrub that grows to about 15 feet in height; produces multiple canelike stems somewhat similar to those of ***Nandina domestica,*** but with foliage to the ground. Dense crown composed of large, glossy, compound leaves; the edges of leaflets undulate characteristically. Flower clusters seem nestled deep within the foliage; blossoms first appear as brilliant red bud clusters in summer and early fall; 6-inch pink flower clusters are composed of many half-inch blossoms. Dome-shaped, 8-inch clusters of purple fruits appear in late fall, turn a brilliant scarlet in winter. Moderate growth rate; easily transplanted.

GROWING CONDITIONS Adaptable; will grow nearly everywhere except near the beach; requires rich, well-watered, well-drained soil; prefers partially shaded locations but will grow in very dense shade, including indoor situations, for extensive periods.

USE Speciment plant; mass planting; container plant; colorful flowers and fruits.

PROPAGATION Easily propagated from seed.

INSECTS/DISEASES None known in Hawai'i.

PRUNING Remove dead or damaged canes to desired height.

FERTILIZING Apply general garden fertilizer (10-30-10) to the planting bed at 3-month intervals, to container plants monthly. Water immediately and thoroughly each time.

DISADVANTAGES None.

Tiliaceae
(Linden Family)

The linden family is composed of 50 genera and about 450 species. Among these are some that provide important products, especially timber and fiber. The lindens are quite similar to members of the hibiscus family (Malvaceae) and the elaeocarpus family (Elaeocarpaceae).

Important species of lindens are jute *(Corchorus olitorius)*, the fibers of which are used in making burlap bags, twine, cloth, and paper; Panama berry *(Muntingia calabura)*, which bears edible fruits and whose bark fibers are fashioned into rope and twine; and trincomalee *(Berrya cordifolia)*, an Indian hardwood used in the construction of houses, boats, and domestic implements. **Four corners *(Grewia occidentalis)*** is the highly ornamental relative described in this book.

Near relatives in the elaeocarpus family are the native Hawaiian kalia *(Elaeocarpus bifidus)*, whose bark and branches were used by Islanders in the construction of thatched houses; and the blue marble tree *(E. grandis)*, an Australian hardwood whose seeds are used for jewelry.

The family takes its name from the genus *Tilia*, which includes the European linden *(Tilia europaea)* and its American cousin, *T. americana*.

Grewia occidentalis
Four Corners, Crossberry, Bow Wood, Buttonwood, Kaffir Hemp

Four corners and crossberry are only two of the many common names given to this plant in its native South Africa. It is so called because its four-parted fruits have a crosslike impression through their centers.

People of the Xhosa tribe fashion the wood into handles for implements and weapons, and warriors of several tribes use the wood for making bows. Branches are plaited into fish traps. Medical uses abound. The Zulus soak the pounded bark in water and apply the infusion to wounds. A tonic, similarly made, is thought to be an aid in childbirth, impotence, and barrenness. Crossberry fruits, like those of most grewias, are said to be edible.

An Indian relative called pharsa *(Grewia asiatica)* has fruits that are made into juice, sherbets, and similar confections. Foremost among the ingenious uses that men have made of the grewias is the production of fibers and cordage from the bark and stems of several species. This is not surprising, for the grewias are closely related to jute, one of the world's great fiber plants.

Crossberry is attaining much popularity in Hawai'i. It is a small, graceful shrub that produces many star-shaped lavender blossoms throughout the year. It is an excellent container plant and good bonsai material. If planted at the top of a retaining wall, its longer branches can hang gracefully over the edge, in much the same way as will a bougainvillea. It is easily trained, withstands severe pruning, and develops interesting gnarled forms.

Grewia is named for Nehemiah Grew (1641–1712), English microscopist and researcher into plant anatomy; *occidentalis* means western.

HABIT A sprawling, woody, evergreen shrub that grows to about 10 feet in height; has a loose crown composed of horizontal, almost pendent, branches. Olive-green, glossy, oval, serrated leaves about 2 inches in length lightly cover the crown. Lavender, star-shaped flowers about 1 inch in diameter appear continuously throughout the year. Small, purple, 4-cornered fruits follow. Slow growth rate; easily transplanted.

GROWING CONDITIONS Very adaptable; prefers cool, moist areas with full sun or partial shade, but will grow in hot, dry areas if constant ground moisture is supplied.

USE Specimen plant; mass planting; container plant; bonsai plant; colorful flowers.

PROPAGATION By seeds or cuttings.

INSECTS/DISEASES For scale, apply malathion or summer oil.

PRUNING Takes well to judicious pruning, assumes attractive regimented forms; may be trained as either an upright or a hanging plant because of the extreme limberness of the branches; may be drastically pruned to induce new growth and flowering.

FERTILIZING Apply general garden fertilizer (10-30-10) to the planting bed at 3-month intervals, and to container plants at monthly intervals. Water immediately and thoroughly after each application.

DISADVANTAGES Flowers sometimes attract wasps.

Malvaceae
(Hibiscus Family)

The name Malvaceae is derived from "mallow," the English rendering of a Latin word, *malva,* itself taken from a Greek term referring to the emollient leaves borne by certain species of plants now included within this family. Among these early mallows is the marsh-mallow *(Althaea officinalis),* the roots of which were used, along with several other materials, in making the first confection bearing the name marshmallow (see p. 94).

Probably the most important subgroup in the hibiscus family comprises species that yield cotton for textiles. Two of these are Sea Island cotton *(Gossypium barbadense)* and tree cotton *(G. arboreum).* A related Hawaiian cotton *(G. sandvicense)* sometimes can be seen growing on the dry, leeward slopes of Hawai'i's major islands. Another native Hawaiian relative is 'ilima *(Sida fallax),* a brilliant yellow- or orange-flowered shrub whose tiny buttercup-like flowers are fashioned by the hundreds into gracefully beautiful leis. The 'ilima is the official flower of the island of O'ahu; it was once the royal flower of the Kamehameha dynasty.

Two relatives brought to Hawai'i by the early Polynesian settlers are milo *(Thespesia populnea),* whose wood was used for construction of houses and containers for food, and whose several parts yielded dyes, medicine, oil, and gum; and hau *(Hibiscus tiliaceus),* whose long, slightly curved, slender branches were made into outriggers for canoes and whose bark provided fibers for a strong cordage, as well as material for making tapa. Gardeners know two other common members of the hibiscus family: a vegetable, okra *(H. esculentus),* and the doorstep flower, hollyhock *(Althaea rosea).*

Hibiscus species are native to both temperate and tropical regions. Generally the plants fall into the herb, shrub, or tree categories. Seventy-five genera and about a thousand species are recognized as members of this considerable family.

The **common hibiscus,** *H. rosa-sinensis,* is the major parent of a great number of present-day hybrids; it is also the basic rootstock for hybrid grafting. Most of the numerous hybrids have been given descriptive names, such as Hawaiian Flag, Kalākaua, Kā'anapali Beauty, Hiwa Hiwa Nani, Kai Nani, and Wai'alae Iki—to name just a few.

Abutilon pictum
Flowering Maple, Painted Abutilon

This plant is not a maple but a mallow, but its leaves have a certain resemblance to those of some genuine maples. Hence the common name.

Flowering maple is tropical in origin, a native of Brazil, and is closely related to Hawai'i's several species of native abutilon. Flowering maple is most valuable for its ornamental beauty, but several relatives have more practical uses. The bark of a close relative in Asia, *Abutilon indicum,* is a source of fiber, while the leaves yield a medicine for treating wounds and a healing lotion for sores. These medicinal properties are known to people from India to the Philippines. Another relative, *Althaea officinalis,* provided material for the ancient confection called marshmallow; the sticky juice extracted from the root was mixed with sugar, gum arabic and egg whites.

In landscaping, flowering maples exhibit colorful foliage and crisp, tissue-thin flowers that hang like papery bells among the branches. Ordinarily they are seen as specimen plants. Although generally not set out in mass plantings, they could be used in that way with striking effect.

Abutilon is an Arabic name for one of the mallows; *pictum,* meaning painted, refers to the brilliantly colored, variegated leaves. Hawaiians call the plant aloalo huamoa, meaning egg hibiscus, because the red-veined, yellow-petaled flowers conjure up an image of a fertilized egg in its shell. They also call it aloalo pele, bell hibiscus, because of its pendent, bell-shaped flowers.

HABIT
An erect, woody, evergreen shrub that grows to about 5 feet in height; has a loose crown with numerous arching branches. Green leaves, about 3 inches in diameter are shaped much like those of maples. Papery yellow and red bell flowers, about 2 inches in diameter, hang from long slender stems. Not known to fruit in Hawai'i. Moderately fast growth rate; easily transplanted; however, because the plant is so readily propagated from cuttings, older specimens are seldom moved.

GROWING CONDITIONS
Adaptable; would grow equally well in cool wet, or hot dry locations; grows best in full sun or light shade; it is not a plant for the beach.

USE
Specimen plant; container plant; colorful flowers.

PROPAGATION
Grown from woody cuttings.

INSECTS/DISEASES
For Chinese rose beetles, apply one of the residual insecticides, such as carbaryl. For thrips, use diazinon or malathion. For scale, spray with malathion or summer oil.

PRUNING
May be pruned to almost any size; prune drastically to encourage new growth, vigorous foliage, dense crown.

FERTILIZING
Apply general garden fertilizer (10-30-10) to the planting bed at 4-month intervals, and to container plants at monthly intervals. Water immediately and thoroughly in each case. In sandy or poor soils, plant is susceptible to deficiencies in minor elements (evidenced by yellowing foliage); use fertilizers containing minor elements, either as foliar sprays or as soil applications, to correct this condition.

DISADVANTAGES
Susceptible to several pests.

Hibiscus acetosella
Purple-leaved Hibiscus

This native of tropical Africa sometimes is confused with its Asian cousin, the roselle *(Hibiscus sabdariffa),* because each produces a thick, juice-filled calyx at the base of its flowers. Juice from the fruits of either plant makes a refreshing drink or a fine jelly for eating with breads or meats. The roselle has further value in that its bark can be processed into rama, a useful jute-like fiber. Several *Hibiscus* species are important fiber plants; the most useful one in Hawai'i is the hau *(H. tiliaceus);* since time immemorial, Hawaiians and other Pacific islanders have used strips of the hau's tough bark for tying and binding.

The purple-leaved hibiscus usually is planted as a specimen. It has rich, red-violet foliage and stems. Flowers, only slightly paler than the foliage, bloom beautifully in the morning hours, then fade quickly during the afternoon. Chinese rose beetles are strongly attracted to the foliage, which suffers massive damage from the greedy insects. This attack can be minimized if the plant is grown where a street lamp or other night lighting helps to inhibit the pests.

Hibiscus is an ancient Greek and Latin name for marsh-mallow, *Althaea officinalis; acetosella* is from *acetum,* Latin for vinegar, and *sella,* Latin for seat, describing the tart sourness of the edible calyces or flower bases.

HABIT
: A sprawling, mounding, evergreen shrub that grows to about 15 feet in height; its loose arching crown is composed of many limber, somewhat weak branches. Red-purple three-lobed foliage distinguishes this plant readily from other species of *Hibiscus.* Flowers, nearly the same shade of purple as the leaves but a bit lighter in intensity, open early in the morning and close by noon; plant blooms continuously throughout the year. Fruits, that also develop throughout the year, split open when mature to discharge seeds. Fast growth rate; easily transplanted.

GROWING CONDITIONS
: Adaptable; grows nearly everywhere in Hawai'i except in extreme beach conditions; requires full sun for best foliage and flowering; becomes very rangy in shade; grows best in rich, well-watered, well-drained soil.

USE
: Specimen plant; mass planting; colorful foliage and flowers.

PROPAGATION
: Grown easily from seeds or cuttings.

INSECTS/DISEASES
: For Chinese rose beetles, apply one of the residual insecticides, such as carbaryl.

PRUNING
: Prune to remove dead or damaged branches; may be pruned heavily to induce new growth and flowering; weak stems and branches should be removed.

FERTILIZING
: Apply general garden fertilizer (10-30-10) to the planting bed at 4-month intervals. Water immediately and thoroughly after each treatment.

DISADVANTAGES
: May be severely attacked by Chinese rose beetles.

Hibiscus rosa-sinensis cv. 'Snowflake'

Common Hibiscus, Chinese Hibiscus, Aloalo, Fu Sang

The common hibiscus, the state flower of Hawai'i, is native to southern China. Today, the hibiscus is almost synonymous with Hawai'i, and here much of the contemporary development of new hybrids takes place. In China, where the plant is named fu sang, and in India, where it is called sapatthu-mal, juice from the flowers is applied to hair and eyebrows to darken them. Juices from the flowers are used as food coloring throughout Asia. The Indian name means shoe-flower: the petals are used to shine shoes. Paper dipped in flower juice becomes blue-violet in color and, like litmus, changes color when acids or alkalies are applied to it. Decoctions of plant parts are thought by Asians to soothe boils and skin tumors.

Hibiscus is the Latin name for several related plants in the genus; *rosa-sinensis,* means literally rose of China. The Hawaiian name is aloalo. The variegated leaf form, commonly called 'Snowflake', is shown here.

HABIT An erect, woody, evergreen shrub, ranging in height from about 3 to 20 feet, and varying in spreading habit and density of foliage, depending on variety; thousands of hybrid varieties exist, all different according to structural, foliar, and floral forms and flower colors. Flowers, 2 to 8 inches across, may be single or double; most last for only one day, but those of some varieties last for two. Blooms best between early fall and late spring. Moderate growth rate; easily transplanted.

GROWING CONDITIONS Very adaptable; will grow almost anywhere, even at the beach, if soil is rich and well watered with good drainage; blooms best in full sun.

USE Specimen plant; mass planting; hedges; container plant; colorful flowers.

PROPAGATION Established hybrids are grafted on common hibiscus rootstock, which is grown from cuttings. New varieties are developed from seeds; during the winter months seeds may be produced by hand pollination early in the morning of the day the flower opens. Remove seeds from pods and plant immediately (seeds will germinate more readily if seedcoat is nicked with a nail file before planting). Snowflake hibiscus must be grown from cuttings.

INSECTS/DISEASES For scale, apply malathion or summer oil. For thrips, aphids, southern green stink-bugs, and mealybugs, use diazinon or malathion. For Chinese rose beetles and hibiscus caterpillars, spray with one of the residual insecticides, such as carbaryl.

PRUNING Prune to shape and remove dead branches in late spring; extensive pruning produces formal, disciplined, but essentially flowerless hedges. If a hybrid plant is grafted on a common hibiscus rootstock, remove any growth from the parent rootstock so that it will not overgrow and weaken the grafted hybrid.

FERTILIZING Apply general garden fertilizer (10-30-10) to the planting bed at 3-month intervals and to container plants monthly; water immediately and thoroughly. In sandy soils, plant is susceptible to deficiencies in minor elements (evidenced by yellowing foliage); apply minor element fertilizers to correct this condition.

DISADVANTAGE Very susceptible to several pests. Overwatering causes premature dropping of buds.

Hibiscus schizopetalus

Coral Hibiscus, Aloalo Ko'ako'a, Fringed Hibiscus,
Arana Gumamela

The coral hibiscus is native to the dry, rocky, coastal hills—and the wet mountain valleys—of tropical East Africa. Sir John Kirk, British physician and diplomat, coexplorer with Dr. David Livingstone, discovered the plant for European horticulture in Mombasa, in what is now Tanzania. For his contributions to scientific discovery, he has been immortalized in the name of the genus *Kirkia* and of more than one hundred species of plants, notably the shrub **Ochna kirkii,** well known in Hawai'i as the **Mickey Mouse plant.**

Coral hibiscus, purely an ornamental plant, is one of the most beautiful species in the genus. Its most remarkable characteristic is its delicately fringed and fluted coral-red flowers, which cascade gracefully from long stems. Coral hibiscus crossed with the **common red hibiscus (Hibiscus rosa-sinensis)** has given us several beautiful hybrids—categorized as butterfly hibiscus.

Hibiscus is the Latin name for related plants in the family (such as hollyhock and marsh-mallow) that were known to early Greeks and Romans; *schizopetalus,* from *schizo,* meaning cut, and *petalon,* meaning a petal, describes the deeply-lobed flower petals. *Ko'a* in Hawaiian is the word for coral, hence the local name, aloalo ko'ako'a.

HABIT An erect, woody, evergreen shrub that grows to about 15 feet in height in a graceful, arching habit. Glossy, dark green leaves with notched edges lightly cover the plant. Pendent, lacy, red-orange to rose flowers, about 3 inches across, hang from long, slender stems. Not known to fruit in Hawai'i. Moderate growth rate; easily transplanted.

GROWING CONDITIONS Very adaptable; will grow nearly everywhere, even near the beach if soil is rich and well watered and the plant is protected from the most extreme salt conditions. Overwatering causes premature bud drop.

USE Specimen plant; mass planting; trimmed or untrimmed hedge; colorful flowers.

PROPAGATION In Hawai'i, where seeds are not formed, propagated always and easily by cuttings.

INSECTS/DISEASES For scale, apply malathion or summer oil. For thrips, aphids, southern green stinkbugs, and mealybugs, use diazinon or malathion (thrips may cause unopened buds to fall). For Chinese rose beetles and hibiscus caterpillars, spray with one of the residual insecticides, such as carbaryl.

PRUNING Prune to shape and to remove dead branches or to reduce size. Plant does not take well to formal shaping because of its weak, pendent branches; should be allowed to grow in a natural arching form.

FERTILIZING Apply general garden fertilizer (10-30-10) to the planting bed at 3-month intervals and to container plants at monthly intervals. Water immediately and thoroughly after each application. In sandy soils, plant is susceptible to deficiencies in minor elements (evidenced by yellowing foliage); apply minor element fertilizers, either as foliar sprays or as additions to soil, to correct this condition.

DISADVANTAGES Very susceptible to several pests.

Hibiscus syriacus
Rose of Sharon, Althaea, Mu Chin, Mukuge, Mu Gung Hwa

Mu gung hwa (eternal flower) is the national flower of Korea. It is native to countries in a wide climatic range, from temperate Korea to tropical Southeast Asia. Chinese know it as Chin or mu Chin, flower of Chin. An ancient Chinese name for Korea was Chin Yüeh, Land of Chin, because of Korea's extensive and age-old cultivation of this plant.

In parts of Asia, leaves are used as a substitute for tea, and the flower petals are considered a vegetable delicacy. Bark fiber is converted into fine papers. A soothing lotion is made from the flowers. A tonic is prepared from the leaves for stomach disorders. The bark and roots provide a remedy for diarrhea and dysentery, and seeds a medicine for headaches and colds.

Hibiscus is the ancient Greek and Latin name for related plants (such as hollyhock and marsh-mallow); *syriacus* is based on a mistake. Linnaeus thought this plant was native to the eastern Mediterranean, not being aware that it had been introduced into Syria from East Asia. Mukuge (beautifully fragrant tree) is a Japanese name.

HABIT
An erect, woody, evergreen shrub in the tropics; in cold climates it loses its leaves in the winter; grows to about 13 feet; has a central trunk with many horizontal branches. Glossy, dark green, notched leaves lightly cover the branches. Single or double, white, cream, pink, or bluish-purple, evening-fragrant flowers appear constantly. Rarely sets seed in Hawai'i. Medium growth rate; easily transplanted.

GROWING CONDITIONS
Grows best in cooler locations where there is consistent rainfall; requires rich, well-watered, well-drained soil; blooms best in full sun.

USE
Specimen plant; mass planting; trimmed or untrimmed hedge; colorful flowers.

PROPAGATION
Seeds, if available, create new color varieties; existing varieties are easily propagated from cuttings or by grafting. The grafting process usually is employed in propagating choice hybrids; use recommended rose of Sharon rootstalks for grafting scions.

INSECTS/DISEASES
For scale, apply malathion or summer oil. For thrips, aphids, southern green stinkbugs, and mealybugs, use diazinon or malathion (thrips may cause unopened buds to fall). For Chinese rose beetles and hibiscus caterpillars, spray with one of the residual insecticides, such as carbaryl.

PRUNING
Prune to shape and to remove dead branches or to reduce infestation by scale insects; takes well to formal pruning, as is done often for topiary work, especially in Japan, or for hedges. If plant is grafted on a rootstock, always remove new shoots growing from below the graft to keep the rootstock from overwhelming it.

FERTILIZING
Apply general garden fertilizer (10-30-10) to the planting bed at 3-month intervals, and to container plants monthly; water immediately and thoroughly. In sandy soils, plant is susceptible to deficiencies in minor elements (evidenced by yellowing foliage); apply fertilizer containing minor elements to correct this condition.

DISADVANTAGES
Very susceptible to several pests; not at its best at low elevations in Hawai'i.

Malvaviscus arboreus
Turk's Cap, Sleeping Hibiscus, Firecracker Hibiscus,
Aloalo Pahūpahū

Turk's cap is native to Central and South America, where it is commonly seen growing in the cool highlands. In Mexico a medicine for relieving sore throat is made from the flowers. As with other species of *Hibiscus*, this plant's bark is composed of tough fibers useful in weaving and in the production of cordage and other ties.

Turk's cap is so named because the flowers resemble the red felt fez that Turkish men and other Muslims formerly wore. The plant is generally called sleeping hibiscus in the South Pacific because of the furled flower's inability to open completely. Hawaiians sometimes call the plant aloalo pahūpahū, or firecracker hibiscus, because the brilliant red flowers look like unexploded firecrackers.

In character and habit, Turk's cap is much like other species of *Hibiscus*. It is an excellent specimen plant, and makes a colorful informal hedge. Flowers constantly brighten the branches. Turk's cap must be grown from cuttings in Hawai'i because it does not produce seeds in the Islands.

Malvaviscus, from *malva*, an old name for the mallow, and *viscus*, meaning sticky, refers to the mucilaginous sap present in this and many other members of the hibiscus family; *arboreus*, meaning like a tree, describes the mature plant's appearance.

HABIT	An erect, woody, evergreen shrub that grows to about 15 feet in height; its loose crown is composed of many upright hairy branches. Leaves are large, hairy, and dark green. Bright red or pale pink unopened hibiscus-like flowers bloom constantly throughout year. Not known to seed in Hawai'i. Fast growth rate; easily transplanted.
GROWING CONDITIONS	Very adaptable; will grow almost anywhere except close to the beach; prefers cool, moist areas and locations with full sun.
USE	Specimen plant; informal hedge; colorful flowers.
PROPAGATION	Propagated from cuttings (young growth will appear on stems before roots develop).
INSECTS/DISEASES	For scale, apply malathion or summer oil. For thrips and mealybugs, use diazinon or malathion. For Chinese rose beetles, spray with one of the residual insecticides, such as carbaryl.
PRUNING	Prune to shape and to remove dead branches; may be vigorously pruned to induce new growth and flowering; not usually trimmed as a formal hedge.
FERTILIZING	Apply general garden fertilizer (10-30-10) to the planting bed at 4-month intervals. Water immediately and thoroughly after each application. In sandy or poor soils, plant is susceptible to deficiencies in minor elements (evidenced by yellowing foliage); to correct this condition, use minor element fertilizers, either as foliar sprays or as soil applications.
DISADVANTAGES	Susceptible to several insect pests.

Theaceae
(Tea Family)

The name Theaceae comes from the Dutch rendering of the dialectical (Amoy) Chinese word *t'e,* for what we refer to as tea. The tea of commerce, made from the leaves of *Thea sinensis,* is native to the warmer parts of southern China, where a number of agricultural cultivars have been selected and grown in great abundance for many centuries. Tea is grown locally only in the cooler, moist Island areas. The entire tea family consists of 16 genera and about 500 species of tropical and subtropical plants, most of which are trees or shrubs.

A native Hawaiian tea relative is ānini *(Eurya sandwicensis),* a forest tree or tall shrub. The white-flowered sasaki *(Cleyera japonica)* is native to the warmer parts of Japan, China, and Korea. It is an evergreen tree, parts of which are used in Shinto rituals in Japan, both at shrines and in homes. Small branches of the sacred sasaki are placed upon household altars for significant occasions. Because sasaki trees are so highly regarded, they are often planted on the grounds of Shinto shrines.

Two colorful relatives of the tea plant, **Camellia japonica** and **Camellia sasanqua,** are among the tea relatives grown in Hawai'i.

Camellia japonica
Common Camellia, Tsubaki, Ch'a Hua, Shan Ch'a, Dong Baeck Gut

The common camellia is native to Japan, where it is called tsubaki (tree of spring); to China, where it is named ch'a hua (tea flower) and shan ch'a (mountain tea); and to Korea, where it is named dong baeck gut (faithfulness). Many varieties of camellias have been cultivated for centuries throughout the Orient, and hundreds of flower varieties have been created. It is most often used in Oriental gardens as a tall background planting. In Korea and Japan a nondrying hair oil is pressed from the plant's seeds. Koreans fashion the hard, closely grained wood into fine furniture.

In Hawai'i camellias usually are planted in gardens in the cool, upper mountain areas, where they bloom beautifully during the winter and spring months. Hawaiian plantings attain only about one-third the height and size of those in temperate Asian gardens, because Island temperatures are too high for optimum growth.

Camellia is named for Georg Josef Kamel (1661–1706), a Jesuit priest from Moravia, who traveled throughout the Ladrones (now the Mariana Islands) and the Philippines, and in 1704 wrote about the plants of Luzon in the appendix to *Historia Plantarum* (under his Latinized name Camellus); *japonica* means from Japan. Hawaiians know the plant as kamila.

HABIT An erect, woody, evergreen shrub that grows to about 15 feet in height at cooler elevations (2,000 to 4,000 feet) in Hawai'i. In warmer and dryer areas, plants grow to less than half that height. Branches angle sharply upward from the main trunk to form a columnar crown. Glossy, leathery, dark green, oval leaves, 2 to 3 inches long, thickly cover the branch tips. Each of the many horticultural varieties has its own distinctive flowers, about 3 to 5 inches in diameter; some are single, others double, crested, or frilled; all are odorless; colors range from white through pinks to reds and combinations of those hues; blooming season October through April. Marble-shaped, 1-inch seedpods follow blooms. Rather slow growth rate; easily transplanted.

GROWING CONDITIONS Does not grow well in extremely hot locations or at the beach; in Hawai'i, prefers cool, moist, upland areas, in sunny or partially shaded locations; requires rich, well-composted, well-watered, well-drained soil.

USE Specimen plant; mass planting; espalier; container plant; colorful flowers.

PROPAGATION Individual varieties must be propagated from cuttings; seeds produce new varieties. Named varieties may be grafted on established rootstocks grown from seeds.

INSECTS/DISEASES For scale, apply malathion or summer oil. Thrips will damage flower buds and prevent them from opening; to control, use diazinon or malathion.

PRUNING May be severely pruned to shape into topiary, bonsai, and espalier forms; responds well to pruning.

FERTILIZING Apply special fertilizers for acid-loving plants at 3-month intervals to the planting bed, and to container plants monthly; water immediately and thoroughly.

DISADVANTAGES Not suitable for use in Hawai'i's lower elevations.

Camellia sasanqua

Sasanqua Camellia, Sazanka, Ch'a Hua, Chan Ch'a, Kamila,
Appleblossom Camellia

Sasanqua camellias are native to China and Japan, where they have been cultivated for hundreds of years. Yunnan Province of southwestern China, where hundreds of varieties were known, was an important center of camellia cultivation. In Japan, sazanka often is planted near teahouses because the plant adds delicate beauty and sweet fragrance to the surroundings. Popular as garden ornamentals, sasanqua camellias were also cultivated for their seeds. The oil expressed from these seeds (tea seed oil) was a valuable product used in textile production and in the manufacture of soap, as well as for dressing the hair of people who could afford to buy it. Refined tea seed oil is edible and can be used in cooking. The Chinese know the plant as ch'a hua (tea flower) and chan ch'a (mountain tea).

Camellia is named for Georg Josef Kamel (1661–1706), a Jesuit priest from Moravia, who traveled through the Ladrones (now the Mariana Islands) and the Philippines; *sasanqua* is derived from sazanka, an old Japanese name for the plant. Hawaiians call it kamila. It is known as appleblossom camellia in Australia.

HABIT An erect, woody, evergreen shrub that grows to about 10 feet in height at cooler elevations (2,000 to 4,000 feet). In warmer and dryer areas, grows to less than half that height. Branching system irregularly upright, giving plant an attractive straggliness. Glossy, leathery, dark green, oval, tooth-edged leaves, 1 to 2 inches in length, sparsely cover the branches. Many horticultural varieties are recognized; one has gold and green striped leaves. Each variety has its own distinctive flowers, each about 2 inches in diameter, single or double, and fragrant; colors range from white through pinks and reds to yellows and combinations of these hues. Blooming season in Hawai'i from October through April. Marble-shaped, ½-inch seedpods follow the blooms. Rather slow growth rate; easily transplanted.

GROWING CONDITIONS Does not grow well in extremely hot locations or at the beach; prefers cool, moist, upland elevations in Hawai'i, where it will grow in sunny or partially shaded locations; requires rich, well-composted, well-watered, well-drained soil.

USE Specimen plant; mass planting; espalier; container plant; colorful flowers.

PROPAGATION Established varieties must be propagated from cuttings; seeds produce new varieties. Named varieties may be grafted upon established seedling rootstocks.

INSECTS/DISEASES For scale, apply malathion or summer oil. Thrips will damage flower buds and prevent them from opening; to control, use diazinon or malathion.

PRUNING May be severely pruned to shape into topiary, bonsai, and espalier forms; responds well to pruning.

FERTILIZING Apply special fertilizers for acid-loving plants at 3-month intervals to the planting bed, to container plants at monthly intervals. Water immediately and thoroughly.

DISADVANTAGES Not suitable for Hawai'i's low elevations.

Ochnaceae
(Ochna Family)

Ochna is a Greek name for a wild pear (*Pyrus* sp.), a member of the **rose family (Rosaceae),** to whose foliage the plants classified in the ochna family bear some resemblance. Forty genera and about 600 species are included in the Ochnaceae. The family consists almost exclusively of plants from the tropics, and most of them are either trees or shrubs.

The **Mickey Mouse plant** *(Ochna kirkii)* is a common ornamental shrub in Hawaiian gardens. A near relative, *O. multiflora,* closely resembling the Mickey Mouse plant, is grown commonly in Southern California gardens but is seldom seen in Hawai'i. Other members of the family are known mostly to botanists—or to people who live near the native habitats of the individual species.

Ochna kirkii
Mickey Mouse Plant

The Mickey Mouse plant makes excellent fence posts in its native tropical East Africa. It has very hard, dense wood which stands up well in that climate. Other *Ochna* species are used for finer kinds of woodwork, wheel spokes, utensil handles, and engraving plates. Oil pressed from the seeds of the Mickey Mouse plant is used by several African tribes for hair dressing. Ochnas also have medicinal properties respected in both Africa and India. In Malabar, a decoction of the leaves and bark of one species is mixed with milk and water as a remedy for stomach disorders and to control vomiting.

The Mickey Mouse plant gets its popular name from its colorful fruits. Bright yellow flowers are followed by an enlarged, vivid red flower base upon which glossy black berries form—like black-eared, red-nosed Mickey Mouse faces peeping out from the leaves of the shrub. Mickey Mouse plant is a trouble-free, well-behaved, easy-to-grow shrub. It is easily trimmed into specific forms, such as an espalier flat against a wall. Even when not in bloom it is an attractive foliage plant.

Ochna, from *ochne*, a Greek name for a wild pear (*Pyrus* sp.), because the leaves resemble those of the pear tree; *kirkii* is named for Sir John Kirk (1832–1922), British physician, naturalist, and diplomat, who accompanied Dr. David Livingstone on his second expedition into Central Africa in 1858. Kirk made large collections of the flora of tropical Africa; more than one hundred species, as well as the genus *Kirkia,* are named for him.

HABIT   An erect, woody, evergreen shrub that grows to about 8 feet in height and has multiple branches and a bushy crown. Glossy, oval, olive-green leaves about 2 inches in length; new growth is slightly pink to bronze. Bright yellow flowers about 1 inch in diameter. After petals fall, base of flower reddens and enlarges; green, turning to black, berry-like fruits are arranged in a ring around the flower base. In Hawai'i, blooms best from spring through summer, but does flower irregularly throughout much of the year. Slow growth rate; easily transplanted.

GROWING CONDITIONS   Adaptable; grows in many locations if planted in rich, well-watered, well-drained soil; prefers cooler, moist locations; blooms well in partial shade; may be planted in sunnier locations if there is much natural cloud cover.

USE   Specimen plant; mass planting; container plant; colorful flowers and fruits.

PROPAGATION   Always propagated from seeds.

INSECTS/DISEASES   For scale, apply malathion or summer oil. For thrips and mealybugs, use diazinon or malathion.

PRUNING   Responds well to considerable pruning.

FERTILIZING   Apply general garden fertilizer (10-30-10) to the planting bed at 3-month intervals, to container plants monthly. Water immediately and thoroughly each time.

DISADVANTAGES   None of importance.

114

Lythraceae
(Crepe Myrtle Family)

The name Lythraceae comes from the Greek word *lythron,* which means gore or black blood, referring to the ruddy colors of many of the flowers borne by species in this family. Twenty-five genera and about 550 species of herbs, shrubs, and trees are classified in the crepe myrtle family. They are native to most of the earth's climatic zones, with the exception of the Arctic regions.

Possibly the plant most commonly used within the family is henna *(Lawsonia inermis);* for many centuries the well-known red dye has been extracted for coloring hair, nails, skin, teeth, leather, and fabrics of silk and wool. Early Chinese and Egyptians used the plant for its dye. In many countries henna is cultivated for its medicinal properties as well.

Hawai'i's most common ornamental relative is the **crepe myrtle *(Lagerstroemia indica).*** In other countries it is sometimes called the itching flower, because when the trunk is rubbed the delicate flowers will tremble on the branches. Crepe myrtles were planted extensively in the gardens of the emperors of the T'ang Dynasty in Peking.

A somewhat larger relative that is native to India and Australia, the tree-sized giant crepe myrtle *(Lagerstroemia speciosa),* is often planted along streets in Hawai'i. In India parts of this plant are used medicinally as a purgative and a relief for fevers.

Cuphea ignea
Cigar Flower, Pua Kīkā

This Mexican plant is one of a very large group of relatives native to North and South America. More than 250 species of *Cuphea* are known. One of these, *C. glutinosa,* from Brazil and Argentina, has leaves that are used in the preparation of medicines for treating intestinal disorders. The leaves have perspiration-inducing qualities also.

The cigar flower appears to have ornamental use only. Its name perfectly describes the flowers' resemblance to tiny, ash-tipped cigars. In Hawai'i, pua kīkā (cigar flowers) are strung into exquisite leis; more than 2,000 flowers are needed to make each lei. Flowers, strung crosswise through their sides, are so arranged on the thread that their red bases and white tips produce brilliant spiral patterns in the thick garland. This is indeed a lei for very special occasions. It can last one month if refrigerated when not in use.

In the garden, the shrub in bloom is brightly colorful. It is a small, low, rounded plant, very suitable for borders and foreground color accents. When not in bloom, it has little visual effect and retreats somewhat into the background, overshadowed by more dramatic or more colorful neighbors.

Cuphea, from *kyphos,* meaning curved, refers to the plant's arched seedpods; *ignea,* meaning fiery red, refers to the flowers' brilliant scarlet hue.

HABIT A low, dense, bushy, rather herbaceous and soft-stemmed, evergreen shrub that grows to a height of about 3 or 4 feet. Small, narrow, dark green leaves densely cover the plant. Narrow tubular flowers, bright orange or pale pink in color, with white lips, bloom at intervals throughout the year. Produces small fruiting capsules containing numerous seeds. Reseeds itself readily in the garden. Individual plants are not long-lived. Fast growth rate; seedlings are transplantable, but mature plants are difficult to transplant successfully.

GROWING CONDITIONS Adaptable; will grow almost anywhere except in extreme salt conditions; prefers cooler, moist areas, constant ground moisture, rich, well-watered, well-drained soil; blooms and grows best in full sun.

USE Specimen plant; mass planting; container plant; colorful flowers.

PROPAGATION Propagated from seeds.

INSECTS/DISEASES None known in Hawai'i.

PRUNING Remove dead and damaged branches only.

FERTILIZING Apply general garden fertilizer (10-30-10) to the planting bed at 3-month intervals and to container plants at monthly intervals. Water immediately and thoroughly after each application.

DISADVANTAGES Individual plants are relatively short-lived, lasting perhaps 2 to 3 years.

Lagerstroemia indica
Crepe Myrtle, Queen Flower, Kāhili Flower, Melindres, Telinga China

This crepe myrtle, a native of China, is one of 25 species given that common name; all of them are found growing naturally throughout parts of Africa, Australia, and Asia. The leaves of this species are a primary food for certain kinds of silkworms. The Japanese use charcoal from the wood as a thickening for some types of lacquer. In Bengal, where the plant is named telinga China, and in other parts of India, the bark is thought to have properties that act as a stimulant and as a reducer of fevers. In Southeast Asia the bark, leaves, and flowers are said to have a purgative effect.

Flower clusters of the crepe myrtle have a cylindrical form similar to that of a Hawaiian kāhili; hence the common names kāhili flower and queen flower by which the plant is known in Hawai'i. Filipinos call the plant melindres, a Spanish word that means a narrow ribbon or fastidiousness.

In cooler climates this crepe myrtle grows into a 30-foot tree, but in Hawai'i it grows as a shrub. Several horticultural varieties are recognized, including a dwarf which grows to little more than a foot in height.

Lagerstroemia is named for Magnus von Lagerstroem (1691–1759), a Swedish friend of Linnaeus, who gave this plant its Latin name; *indica* (from India) was used by Linnaeus to denote either India or China.

HABIT
An erect, vertical, woody, deciduous shrub that grows to about 12 feet in height in Hawai'i, and in cooler climates, to 25 to 30 feet. Medium green, oval leaves, about 1 inch long; leaves take autumn colors in the fall. Large clusters of frilly flowers, in colors ranging from white to pink to red to blue-violet, appear in summer and early fall in Hawai'i. Woody seedpods follow in winter, split open, and release small flat seeds. Moderate growth rate; easily transplanted.

GROWING CONDITIONS
Adaptable; prefers hot, full sun conditions and rich, well-watered, well-drained soil; becomes attenuated in the shade.

USE
Specimen plant; mass planting; colorful flowers; the dwarf variety is an excellent container plant.

PROPAGATION
Color varieties are propagated by cuttings; seedlings produce variable color offspring.

INSECTS/DISEASES
For Chinese rose beetles, apply one of the residual insecticides, such as carbaryl. For powdery mildew, use dusting sulfur. Newly developed varieties are resistant to powdery mildew.

PRUNING
Withstands vigorous pruning to any shape; may be trained into a small tree form; prune drastically to encourage vigorous new growth and a dense crown.

FERTILIZING
Apply general garden fertilizer (10-30-10) to the planting bed at 4-month intervals, and to container plants at monthly intervals. Water immediately and thoroughly after each application.

DISADVANTAGES
Dormant during winter months.

Pemphis acidula
Mikimiki, Mentigi, Kiejor, Kiñe

Mikimiki, as Polynesians call it, can be found growing on the shores of most islands in the Indian Ocean and the tropical Pacific. It is a beach dweller without peer. The sturdy little shrub grows in some of the most inhospitable of conditions at the water's edge. Sometimes it is found growing on solid coral, its roots anchored in the coral's fissures. Mikimiki is so well adapted to ocean conditions that it can grow even when partly covered by salt water. Pacific islanders have found the dense hard wood to be highly useful for making tool and weapon handles, pegs, small dishes for food, and storage containers for small articles. Mikimiki's naturally angular branches require little carving to be converted into strong, curved fishhooks. Its tart leaves are quite edible.

Aside from its ability to grow nearly anywhere at the beach, mikimiki is a good choice for hot, sunny locations in gardens. It takes extremely well to pot culture; its picturesque branching habit gives it an immediate bonsai appearance. Mikimiki is less happy in extremely shady areas; without substantial sunshine its crisp, gray-green leaves turn to a listless green.

Pemphis, meaning breath, or filled with air, or a bubble, refers to the bubble-shaped cap covering the seedpod; *acidula,* meaning acid or sour, refers to the taste of the edible leaves. Malaysians call the plant mentigi; Marshall Islanders give it two names, kiejor and kiñe.

HABIT — A sprawling, woody, evergreen shrub that grows to about 4 feet in height. Small gray-green leaves, about ¾ inch long, are arranged picturesquely along the tough little branches; lower branches become bare as leaves turn yellow and fall. Small, ½-inch, cup-shaped flowers bloom irregularly throughout the year. Flowers are followed by tiny reddish fruits that become brown with age; seed capsule is covered by a tiny domed cap; capsule contains minute, dust-like seeds. Very slow growth rate; easily transplanted unless roots have become established in rocky locations.

GROWING CONDITIONS — Very adaptable; will withstand some of the worst of ocean shore conditions; although it prefers an alkaline soil, will grow inland in almost any type of soil, as long as it is well drained; requires full sun, prefers hot beach conditions.

USE — Specimen plant; mass planting; excellent container plant and bonsai.

PROPAGATION — Grown from seeds.

INSECTS/DISEASES — None of importance.

PRUNING — Naturally takes a picturesque spreading form; requires little pruning except to shape or to remove occasional straggly growth.

FERTILIZING — Apply a small amount of general garden fertilizer (10-30-10) to the planting bed at yearly intervals, and smaller amounts to container plants, also at yearly intervals. Water immediately and thoroughly after each application.

DISADVANTAGES — None.

Punicaceae
(Pomegranate Family)

The pomegranate family is one of the smallest of all plant families; it contains only one genus, *Punica,* which has only two species. In ancient times, pomegranate *(P. granatum)* was called malum punicum or the Punic apple. *Punica* is derived from Greek and Latin terms referring to the Phoenicians, who founded the city-state of Carthage near the site of present-day Tunis.

In China the pomegranate is named shih liu, which means stone tumor, alluding to the appearance of the fruit. Pomegranates have been symbols of fruitfulness and prolific life for centuries, because their many seeds are highly viable and sprout readily. The pomegranate is the national emblem of Spain.

Botanically speaking, pomegranate fruits are actually berries furnished with thick leathery rinds that cover the juicy coats of the many seeds borne within.

Punica granatum var. *nana*

Dwarf Pomegranate, Pomekelane, Pomaikalana, Granada, Apple of Carthage

The pomegranate *(Punica granatum)* is one of the oldest fruits of commerce. For the people of many different cultures it has long been a symbol of good fortune, fertility, and immortality. This symbolism is founded in the capacity of a single plant to produce thousands of viable seeds, thus assuring the constant regeneration of the line.

The shrub has many medicinal and cosmetic uses: the flowers provide a dye for hair; leaves and flowers yield potions for gargling; the astringent fruit peel and fresh root have tonic properties that aid in the treatment of severe digestive and intestinal disorders. The flavorful fruit produces large amounts of cooling juice, which may be allowed to ferment into a delicious wine. Grenadine syrup is made from pomegranate fruit.

Although the dwarf pomegranate *(P. granatum* var. *nana)* produces many small edible fruits, it is grown mainly for its colorful foliage and flowers, planted as a specimen or in small groups. It is also a fine container plant.

Punica has preserved the very old Latin name for the plant, *malum punicum,* which means apple of Carthage. *Punica* is derived from Poeni, an ancient name for the Phoenician ancestors of the Carthaginians; *granatum,* meaning having many seeds, accurately describes the fruit; *nana,* meaning dwarf, differentiates the smaller variety from its larger parent. Pomekelane and pomaikalana are Hawaiian derivatives of the English name.

HABIT An erect, woody shrub that grows to about 6 or 8 feet in height; the loose crown shows the trunk and branching system; the weight of the fruits causes branch tips to weep. Glossy, narrow, light green leaves are about 2 inches long; foliage is sometimes reddish. Cultivated varieties exhibit red, white, pink, or yellow flowers by distinctive rosy-cheeked pomegranates about 1½ inches in diameter. Produces flowers and fruits constantly throughout the year. Moderate growth rate; easily transplanted.

GROWING CONDITIONS Very adaptable; will grow almost anywhere in Hawai'i except in extreme salt conditions; prefers rich, well-watered, well-drained soil in sunny locations; becomes attenuated in shade. Will resist some drought, but then is subject to partial dieback.

USE Specimen plant; mass planting; hedging; container plant; bonsai.

PROPAGATION Established varieties are grown from cuttings, new varieties from seed.

INSECTS/DISEASES For scale, apply summer oil.

PRUNING May be pruned vigorously to shape.

FERTILIZING Apply general garden fertilizer (10-30-10) to the planting bed at 3-month intervals, and to container plants at monthly intervals. Water immediately and thoroughly after every application. Brown leaf tips indicate phosphorous deficiency; add superphosphate fertilizer to planting bed or container in 2 applications, 2 months apart, to correct this condition. Yellowish leaves indicate iron deficiency; use foliar fertilizers containing iron, in one application, to correct this condition.

DISADVANTAGES None.

126

Combretaceae
(Terminalia Family)

The name Combretaceae is derived from *combretum,* a Latin word for certain climbing members of this family. The terminalia family includes 20 genera and about 600 species, most of which are tropical and subtropical trees, shrubs, and vines. The common name of the family is that of the genus *Terminalia,* which includes Hawai'i's well known beach tree, the false kamani *(T. catappa).* This colorful tree, native to Indonesia's shores, is known as the tropical almond throughout much of the Pacific region. It is an important plant: the wood is cut into timber for boats and houses; the almond-like fruits, besides being edible, produce dyes; and several parts of the tree yield an excellent tanning agent.

Another popular ornamental relative, the silver buttonwood *(Conocarpus erectus* var. *sericeus),* is a native of the Caribbean. The several parts of this plant are used in the Caribbean in much the same way as those of the false kamani are used in the Pacific islands. Two ornamental vine relatives grown in Hawai'i are the Rangoon creeper *(Quisqualis indica)* and combretum *(Combretum grandiflorum).*

The **dwarf geometry tree** *(Bucida spinosa)* is a natural bonsai shrub. Its larger relative, the geometry tree *(B. buceras),* is seen in many Hawaiian gardens.

Bucida spinosa
Dwarf Geometry Tree

Hawai'i's first dwarf geometry trees were sent to Foster Botanic Garden from Florida's Fairchild Tropical Garden in 1964. The tiny shrubs achieved instant popularity in Hawai'i. Now hundreds of seedlings from these first plants are growing in gardens throughout the Islands. The dwarf geometry tree's big brother, *Bucida buceras,* is a well-known source of timber in the Caribbean and one of Hawai'i's many interesting ornamental trees. In tropical America, its strong and durable wood, being resistant to dry-wood termites, is often used for making houses and fences, flooring, scaffolding for heavy construction, workbenches, railroad ties, and pilings. The bark yields a useful tanning agent. Medicinally, bark from the geometry tree and from the mangrove *(Rhizophora mangle)* are mixed and processed into a styptic agent.

The dwarf geometry tree is a very picturesque plant, delicately small in scale. Each plant assumes its own distinctive appearance. The characteristically horizontal branches, when matured, assume extremely beautiful windblown forms. It is among the best of Hawai'i's container plants, and it is also one of the most popular new plants available to bonsai craftsmen.

Bucida, from *buc,* meaning ox, and *oides,* the suffix meaning like, refers to an interesting condition that develops in the seedpods of plants in this genus. Sometimes in the Caribbean mites will attack a seedpod, creating a gall; the abnormal, horn-shaped pod swells to become 8 to 10 times larger than the normal ¼-inch seedpods. The resemblance of the enlarged pod to an ox head, gives the genus its name; *spinosa* means thorny or prickly.

HABIT A small, low, picturesque, spreading, partially deciduous shrub that grows to about 4 feet in height; distinctive branching system, strongly horizontal, gives the plant a layered appearance, almost a natural bonsai in shape. Tiny, bright, light green leaves are about ¼ inch long; new foliar growth is bronze-colored and turns with age to light green; stems are very spiny. Insignificant flowers are followed by clusters of tiny brown fruits; bears flowers and fruits periodically throughout the year. Slow growth rate; easily transplanted.

GROWING
CONDITIONS Very adaptable; will grow almost anywhere except in extreme salt conditions, but plant will lose its foliage and languish in dense shade; grows best in rich, well-watered, well-drained soil and in full sun; an excellent container plant.

USE Specimen plant; rock garden plant; container plant; bonsai.

PROPAGATION Sometimes plant is grown commercially, with great difficulty, from cuttings; better results are gained with seeds, but germination is very poor. Use fresh, mature seeds.

INSECTS/DISEASES None in Hawai'i.

PRUNING Naturally a picturesque plant which does not require much pruning; however, it may be pruned to accentuate its natural shape.

DISADVANTAGES Dormant for short periods each year.

Melastomataceae
(Melastoma Family)

The term *melastoma* comes from the Greek words, *melos,* meaning black, and *stoma,* meaning mouth, and accurately describes the stained mouths of those who eat the berries of certain plants belonging to this family. The melastomas comprise a rather large family, having 240 genera and about 3,000 species, all native to the world's tropics and subtropics. Representatives of the family may be found among several of the plant categories: herbs, shrubs, vines, trees, water and marsh plants, and epiphytes. The family members generally are easily recognized by their leaves, which usually show three distinct, longitudinal veins curving from the base toward the tip.

Aside from **Medinilla magnifica,** the lush, tropical shrub described in this book, probably the most common ornamental melastoma seen in Hawai'i is the colorful groundcover from Africa, *Dissotis rotundifolia.* Three other melastomas originally brought to Hawai'i as ornamentals have escaped from cultivation and now are weedy interlopers in the moist upland regions. They are the very colorful, royally purple princess flower *(Tibouchina urvilleana),* a native of Brazil seen almost everywhere along the roadsides leading from Hilo to the Volcanoes National Park on the Big Island; Koster's curse *(Clidemia hirta),* a brilliant green-leaved weed now covering many mountain slopes on O'ahu and Moloka'i; and the Indian rhododendron *(Melastoma malabathricum),* which has become naturalized on all the main islands, especially on Kaua'i.

Medinilla magnifica

Medinilla, Kapa-kapa

Species of *Medinilla* may be found growing in much of tropical Asia and Africa, and in many islands of the South Pacific. One from Southeast Asia, an epiphytic shrub named *M. hasseltii,* has edible leaves. When young, these leaves are combined with rice and certain small sour fruits in a preparation that is eaten with fish in Sumatran and Javanese foods. Leaves of this species are used also in Indonesia as poultices for headaches. Probably the most spectacular of all the members in this genus is *M. magnifica,* one of 107 species native to the Philippine Islands. Kapa-kapa, as the plant is called in the Tagalog language, appears to be strictly ornamental in use.

Kapa-kapa fulfills its ornamental role gloriously: it is one of Hawai'i's most exotically beautiful landscape plants. Its dark green, heavily veined foliage creates an elegant background for the immense, hanging clusters of brilliant pink and yellow flowers that flush from the plant in spring and summer. For sheer spectacle, this shrub rivals the most colorful gingers and heliconias that Hawai'i offers. Its one disadvantage is that it must be grown only in the most lush, moist locations, thereby severely restricting its use in landscaping. Regrettably, most residential areas on Hawai'i's dry, leeward slopes do not give the plant its needed rain forest environment.

Medinilla is named for José de Medinilla y Pineda, governor of the Ladrones (or Mariana Islands) in 1820; *magnifica* describes the magnificent panicles of flowers.

HABIT An erect, woody, evergreen shrub that grows to about 10 feet in height; the loose crown is composed of angular, pendent branches. Large, leathery, glossy, dark green leaves are about 1 foot long and show prominent longitudinal venation. Hanging clusters of watermelon-pink flowers are surrounded by pale pink bracts; flower clusters, about 18 inches in length, appear during spring and summer. Small purple berries follow the bloom. Slow growth rate; easily transplanted.

GROWING CONDITIONS Grows best in cool, moist areas, in rich soil; requires partial shade and full protection from wind.

USE Specimen plant; mass planting; colorful flowers.

PROPAGATION Most easily grown from seeds, but may also be propagated by cuttings, which is best done in mist-boxes.

INSECTS/DISEASES For scale, apply malathion or summer oil. For mealybugs, use diazinon or malathion.

PRUNING Prune to shape and to remove old flower clusters and damaged foliage.

FERTILIZING Apply general garden fertilizer (10-30-10) to the planting bed at 4-month intervals. Water immediately and thoroughly after each application.

DISADVANTAGES Highly susceptible to damage by wind and falling debris from trees.

134

Araliaceae
(Panax Family)

The family derives its name from *aralia,* a term used to describe several closely related plants. Commercially, the most important of the aralias is ginseng *(Panax quinquefolium),* a native of North America, which has gained widespread use as the source of a medicinal tonic for many Asian peoples. The Asian ginseng, *P. schinseng,* native to Manchuria and Korea, was probably the original source of this tonic. The North American species was introduced later to the commercial scene, but was not as highly prized as was *P. schinseng.*

Fifty-five genera and about 700 species are included in the panax family, most of them native to Indo-Malaysia, tropical America, and the South Pacific islands. Relatives from temperate zones are also abundant, however. This cool-weather group includes many of the ivy species classified in the genus *Hedera.*

Hawai'i's most common ornamental aralias are members of the genus *Polyscias,* several of which are described in this book. Another ornamental aralia common to Hawai'i is the Queensland umbrella tree or octopus tree, *Schefflera actinophylla*—until fairly recently, known as *Brassaia actinophylla.* This Australian plant is often seen in Hawaiian gardens full grown as a major tree, but also as a bonsai rooted upon a stone in a small pot. A rather recent introduction to Hawai'i, the **dwarf umbrella tree *(Schefflera arboricola),*** is discussed in this book.

Another ornamental import to Hawai'i is the rice-paper plant *(Tetrapanax papyriferum);* in its native China its stem pith is shaved into thin spirals and pressed into papery sheets. Yatsude *(Fatsia japonica),* a luxuriant-leaved ornamental shrub from Japan, and English ivy *(Hedera helix)* have been hybridized to produce the handsome vine, fatshedera *(× Fatshedera × lizei).*

Polyscias filicifolia cv. 'Golden Prince'
Golden Prince Panax, Yellow Angelica

Golden Prince panax is a color form of *Polyscias filicifolia,* a very green, feathery panax of South Pacific island origin. In the New Hebrides and other Melanesian islands, the leaves of the parent are boiled and eaten with salt, pepper, and butter. The flavor of this cooked vegetable is somewhat like that of spinach. *P. filicifolia* is commonly called angelica throughout the tropics, somewhat confusingly so, inasmuch as angelica is a name also given to another plant, *Angelica archangelica,* a kitchen herb in the parsley family. Golden Prince is the Hawaiian commercial name for the yellow-leaved form.

Golden Prince panax and its green parent are excellent specimen plants, prized for their foliage. Both forms easily adapt to life in containers and grow readily and healthily for years without repotting. Golden Prince panax is an especially good house plant if it receives average window light. Its foliage, either in the house or in deep shade, is a light chartreuse color. Like most kinds of panax, these two plants are tall, slender shrubs that fit well in narrow garden areas and small planting beds.

Polyscias, from *poly,* meaning many, and *skias,* meaning shade, refers to the group's abundant, shade-producing foliage; *filicifolia,* fern leaf, is from *filicium,* meaning fern, and *folium,* meaning a leaf.

HABIT   An erect, vertical, evergreen, woody shrub that grows to about 15 feet in height; several vertical stems form a light, airy, open crown composed of sparsely placed fern-like leaves. Individual leaves are about 2 feet long, and leaflets, very incised, about 6 to 8 inches. Insignificant flowers in large, unattractive, clusters appear occasionally. Small black fruits follow. Moderate growth rate; easily transplanted.

GROWING CONDITIONS   Adaptable; will grow in most areas except in extreme salt conditions; does well in either full sun, where it produces its most colorful yellow foliage, or in partial or full shade, where the foliage is a light green. Requires rich, well-watered, well-drained soil. Leaves turn brown and fall if plant is not consistently watered.

USE   Specimen plant; mass planting; hedging; container plant; colorful foliage.

PROPAGATION   Propagated by woody cuttings. Cuttings should always be planted upright, never at an angle with the ground; diagonal planting produces ugly, club-footed stems.

INSECTS/DISEASES   Usually insect-free. Bacterial leaf spot sometimes attacks varieties with broader leaves, but does not seem to trouble this species. For aphids, apply diazinon or malathion.

PRUNING   Prune to shape and to remove unwanted stems; plant may be drastically cut back to reduce size and to make it bushier at the base. Remove unattractive flower heads.

FERTILIZING   Apply general garden fertilizer (10-30-10) to the planting bed at 3-month intervals, and to container plants at monthly intervals. Water immediately and thoroughly after each application.

DISADVANTAGES   None. Contrary to popular belief, panax plants are no more subject to termite infestation than are any other woody shrubs.

Polyscias fruticosa
Parsley Panax

Parsley panax has many uses throughout its native habitat, from India to southern Polynesia. The Javanese and Malaysians use parsley panax leaves as a condiment and herb to flavor meats and fish, much as Westerners use kitchen parsley *(Petroselinum crispum)* and celery *(Apium graveolens)*. In Java a decoction of this panax's parsley-scented roots and leaves is considered to be diuretic and is employed in the treatment of kidney stones. In Cambodia and India the astringent, sweat-inducing root is used to treat fevers. Cambodians apply parts of the plant externally for relief of neuralgia and rheumatism. Filipinos sprinkle a healing mixture of powdered leaves and salt upon wounds. Fijians attribute medicinal qualities to the bark. In the Philippines, the foliage is wound into bases for floral wreaths.

Parsley panax is a superior potted plant, having the ability to live robustly in one container for many years. It is an excellent indoor plant, requiring only indirect light from nearby windows. In the mainland nursery trade, the plants are sometimes called—and sold as—"Ming trees"; as such, the small, rooted cuttings are planted in tiny pots and trained in bonsai fashion.

Polyscias, from *poly,* meaning many, and *skias,* meaning shade, refers to the group's abundant, shade-producing foliage; *fruticosa* means shrubby.

HABIT
An erect, evergreen, woody shrub that grows to about 12 feet in height; several vertical stems form a dense, bushy crown of frilly, parsley-like leaflets; total effect is rather airy and lacy. Individual leaflets are highly incised and crinkly; leaves are about 6 inches long; each leaflet 1 to 1½ inches across. Insignificant flowers in large, unattractive, clusters appear occasionally. Small black fruits follow. Moderate growth rate; easily transplanted.

GROWING CONDITIONS
Adaptable; will grow in most areas except in extreme salt conditions; does well in full sun, partial shade, or full shade; foliage tends to be lighter in color in sunnier locations; requires rich, well-watered, well-drained soil. Leaves turn yellow, then brown, and will fall if plants are inadequately watered.

USE
Specimen plant; mass planting; hedging; screening; container plant.

PROPAGATION
Propagated by woody cuttings. Cuttings should always be planted upright, never at an angle with the ground; diagonal planting produces ugly, club-footed stems.

INSECTS/DISEASES
Usually insect-free. Bacterial leaf spot sometimes attacks kinds of panax with broader leaves, but does not affect this species. For aphids, apply diazinon or malathion.

PRUNING
Prune to shape and to remove unwanted stems; plant may be drastically cut back to reduce the size and to rejuvenate the plant, making it bushier at the base. Constantly remove yellow leaves that naturally appear, and remove unattractive flower heads.

FERTILIZING
Apply general garden fertilizer (10-30-10) to the planting bed at 3-month intervals, and to container plants at monthly intervals. Water immediately and thoroughly.

DISADVANTAGES
None. Contrary to popular belief, panax plants are no more subject to termite infestation than are any other woody shrubs.

Polyscias guilfoylei cv. 'Dowsett Crispa'
Dowsett's Curly Panax

This perky shrub can best be described in the vernacular as "a chip off a chip off the old block." Botanically, Dowsett's curly panax is a cultivar of the well-known curly panax which is a cultivar of Hawai'i's common hedge panax, *Polyscias guilfoylei.* The hedge panax, a native of the tropical South Pacific, has been planted in Hawaiian gardens for many decades. Here and elsewhere, leaf variations have been discovered that are very different from those of the parent plant. Whereas leaves of hedge panax are large, oval, irregularly toothed, and very flat, those of curly panax and the Dowsett cultivar are small, tightly contorted, curled, and crinkled. Dowsett's curly panax differs from its immediate parent in that its leaves, although spaced farther apart on the stems, are much more tightly curled and distorted.

Polyscias, from *poly,* meaning many, and *skias,* meaning shade, refers to the group's abundant, shade-producing foliage; *guilfoylei* is named for W. R. Guilfoyle (1840–1912), British-born director of the botanic gardens, Melbourne, Australia. The cultivar, locally, has been named Dowsett's curly panax because it first appeared in the garden of Mr. and Mrs. Herbert M. Dowsett on O'ahu. Sometimes *P. guilfoylei* is erroneously called a coffee tree because of its vague resemblance to the true coffee plant, *Coffea arabica.*

HABIT | A very erect, evergreen, woody shrub that grows to about 8 feet in height; multiple bare stems support a sparse crown of foliage at the upper tips. Tightly curled, stiff, crisp, dark green leaves are about 8 inches in length; individual leaflets, about 1½ inches. Insignificant flowers in large, rather unattractive, clusters appear occasionally. Small black fruits follow. Very slow growth rate; easily transplanted.

GROWING CONDITIONS | Very adaptable; will grow in most areas except in extreme salt conditions; will grow in full sun, partial shade, full shade, or in interior spaces affording only artificial lighting; requires rich, well-watered, well-drained soil. Leaves turn yellow and fall if plant is inadequately watered.

USE | Specimen plant; container plant; indoor plant.

PROPAGATION | Propagated by woody cuttings. Cuttings should always be planted upright, never at an angle with the ground; diagonal planting produces ugly, club-footed stems.

INSECTS/DISEASES | Usually free from insects and diseases. Aphids sometimes attack the new growth of this plant; apply diazinon or malathion.

PRUNING | Individual stems may be pruned to induce foliar growth lower on the plant. Plant requires little pruning, makes its own picturesque shape.

FERTILIZING | Apply general garden fertilizer (10-30-10) to the planting bed at 3-month intervals, and to container plants at monthly intervals. Water immmediately and thoroughly.

DISADVANTAGES | This plant, being a cultivar of the common hedge panax, may revert to that parent form. Contrary to popular belief, panax plants are no more subject to termite infestation than are other woody shrubs.

Polyscias scutellarium cv. 'Pennockii'
Pennock's Panax

Polyscias scutellarium is native to New Caledonia's warm lush forests. The parent shrub, introduced to Puerto Rico, was cultivated at Pennock Brothers' Nursery, where sports—that is, shoots differing in foliage from that of the parent—developed unexpectedly. Pennock Brothers propagated the sports, thereby introducing to the world's nursery trade a new and highly decorative plant, the cultivar 'Pennockii.'

The parent is a very attractive shrub with large, dark green, tooth-edged leaves. Pennock's panax, the more colorful offspring, is highly variegated and very light in color. It is nicely used in shady garden areas and indoor planters; its light, crisp foliage lends bright color accents.

Polyscias, from *poly*, meaning many, and *skias*, meaning shade, refers to the group's abundant shade-producing foliage; *scutellarium*, from the Latin *scutella*, a small shield, describes the shape of the leaves.

HABIT A very erect, vertical, evergreen, woody shrub that grows to about 8 feet in height; has multiple stems; branches initially grow vertically, then tend to sprawl outward; crown is a series of loosely mounded stems and leaves, often quite dense at the top and rather bare at the bottom. Crinkled and scalloped, rounded leaflets, each about 4 to 6 inches in diameter; several leaflets per leaf; insignificant unattractive flowers in large clusters appear occasionally as plant matures. Small black fruits follow. Moderate growth rate; easily transplanted.

GROWING CONDITIONS Adaptable; will grow in most areas except in extreme salt conditions; does not produce good foliage either in full sun or in full shade; does well in filtered sunlight; requires rich, well-watered, well-drained soil. Plants will lose their leaves if inadequately watered.

USE Specimen plant; mass planting; hedging; container plant.

PROPAGATION Propagated by woody cuttings. Cuttings should always be planted upright, never at an angle with the ground; diagonal planting produces ugly, club-footed stems.

INSECTS/DISEASES Generally insect-free. Occasionally, dark brown spots appear on the leaves; this is evidence of bacterial leaf spot; control with applications of Maneb and tribasic copper sulfate solutions. For aphids, apply diazinon or malathion.

PRUNING Prune to shape and to remove unwanted stems and unattractive flower clusters; plant may be drastically cut back to reduce its size and to rejuvenate it; pruning makes it bushier at the base and prevents flowers, which spoil the appearance.

FERTILIZING Apply general garden fertilizer (10-30-10) to the planting bed at 3-month intervals, and to container plants at monthly intervals. Water immediately and thoroughly after each application.

DISADVANTAGES None. Contrary to popular belief, panax plants are no more subject to termite infestation than are any other woody shrubs.

144

Schefflera arboricola
Dwarf Umbrella Tree

This rather recent introduction to Hawai'i is native to Taiwan's neighboring Hainan Island and to parts of Taiwan itself. In nature, it is creeping and vinelike, growing epiphytically on trees. Its closest relative, commonly found growing in Hawaiian gardens, is the Queensland umbrella tree, *Schefflera actinophylla,* a look-alike but a much larger and more treelike plant. In its native Taiwanese forests, the dwarf umbrella seedling begins its growth on the branches of a large tree, then sends down abundant and aggressive roots which derive nourishment from the variety of organic substances present on the host plant's bark. The dwarf umbrella tree is not a parasite, however, and does not rob the host tree of its strength and nourishment; however, it may in time overshade its host, thereby weakening it.

In Hawai'i the plant is almost always grown in soil, as specimen material or in low hedges, or especially in pots. One somewhat unnerving problem associated with trying to grow this plant in the garden develops from the fact that its wide-ranging roots will escape from a pot and grow along lanais and terraces to invade neighboring containers. Periodic root pruning is required. Several Hawaiian nurseries send thousands of rooted dwarf umbrella tree cuttings annually to greenhouse owners overseas; these plants are sold as potted material for indoor decoration in cold-climate areas.

Schefflera is named for J. C. Scheffler, nineteenth-century botanist, of Danzig; *arboricola,* from *arboris,* meaning tree, and the suffix *-cola,* meaning dweller, refers to the plant's natural habitat, the crowns of forest trees.

HABIT An erect, woody, evergreen shrub that grows to about 18 feet in height and has a loose, open branching system and an aggressive root system. Glossy, medium green, leathery, finger-like leaves appear at the ends of the long stems; usually bases of stems are bare. Not known to flower and fruit in Hawai'i. Rapid growth rate; extremely easy to transplant.

GROWING CONDITIONS Very adaptable; will grow nearly anywhere in Hawai'i except in extreme salt conditions; will grow in nearly any type of soil; grows well in full sunny locations, but produces darker green and more lush foliage in partially shaded areas.

USE Specimen plant; pruned hedge; container plant.

PROPAGATION Grown from cuttings.

INSECTS/DISEASES For scale, apply malathion or summer oil. For mealybugs, use diazinon or malathion.

PRUNING May be severely pruned to induce heavy foliage and compactness; if a more open plant is desired, little pruning is necessary.

FERTILIZING Apply general garden fertilizer (10-30-10) to the planting bed at 4-month intervals, to container plants monthly. Water immediately and thoroughly each time.

DISADVANTAGES Plant has a very aggressive root system and may work itself into areas where it is not wanted. Roots sometimes grow through the drainage hole in the plant's container.

146

Ericaceae
(Heath Family)

Erica is an ancient Greek name for heath. Representatives of the heath family are distributed throughout much of the world, especially in the cool tropical upland and temperate regions. Fifty genera and about 1,350 species are known. Heaths often are community plants; that is, they grow in widespread communal assemblages, such as the heaths of the British Isles, the cranberry bogs of the American Atlantic coast, and the azalea-resplendent swamps of the American southeast. Some of these communal associations are considered to be among the oldest of ecosystems. Probably the most interesting commercial heaths are briarwood *(Erica arborea)* and bruyère *(E. scoparia)* whose dense, marbled roots provide the raw materials for the best kinds of pipes for smoking tobacco. The heaths and sphagnum moss are the plants primarily responsible for the ages-old deposits of vegetable material in bogs and marshes that ultimately become peat.

The heath family includes the cranberry and also the blueberry and huckleberry, all of which are *Vaccinium* species. A native Hawaiian heath closely related to these popular berries is the 'ōhelo *(V. reticulatum)*, the bush that, growing as it does near Kīlauea volcano, is sacred to Pele, goddess of the volcano. Faithful Hawaiians, before eating 'ōhelo berries, throw some of them or whole branches of the plant, into her volcanoes to placate the fiery goddess.

Ornamental relatives from the temperate zone, many of which are native to North America, include the heaths and heathers (*Erica* spp.), the rhododendrons and azaleas (*Rhododendron* spp.), mountain laurel *(Kalmia latifolia)*, madrone *(Arbutus menziesii)*, bigberry manzanita *(Arctostaphylos glauca)*, and bearberry *(A. uva-ursi)*. The **Indian azalea *(Rhododendron indicum)***, a Japanese heath, is described in this book.

Rhododendron indicum
Azalea, Satsuki-tsutsuji

This species of azalea, a native of Japan, is one of that country's most popular and useful garden ornamentals. Called satsuki-tsutsuji in Japanese, the plant is used most often in masses of clipped, mounded forms suggesting the large rounded stones along a stream bed. Although azaleas are primarily ornamental, several relatives have medicinal uses. *Rhododendron chrysanthum,* an Indian shrub, has leaves that are prescribed in the treatment of gout and rheumatism. Leaves of *R. ferrugineum,* a native of the European Alps, contain toxic and narcotic substances that are deadly to sheep and goats, and yet a derived medicine is used—with extreme care—for human patients, as a diuretic, a sudorific, and a depurative.

Azaleas generally are seen as small, densely foliaged shrubs planted singly or in groups in garden borders and, especially in Hawai'i, in Oriental-style rock gardens. They are also used extensively as container plants, often for the color of their flowers, in somewhat the same manner as are bougainvilleas. Some varieties bear a few flowers sporadically all year long, but for most azaleas the peak blooming season in Hawai'i is late fall to early spring.

Rhododendron, from *rhodon,* meaning rose, and *dendron,* meaning tree, is a name used by classical writers for oleander *(Nerium oleander),* an entirely unrelated plant. Linnaeus, the eighteenth-century Swedish botanist, called this particular plant *Azalea indica,* but a later British botanist, Robert Sweet, renamed it *Rhododendron indicum.* The term *indica* was used rather loosely by Linnaeus for the native habitats of plants from both China and India.

HABIT An erect, woody, evergreen shrub that grows to about 5 feet in height. Spreading, woody branches are covered with a dense mass of small, oval, hairy leaves about 1 inch long. Flowers, 2 to 3 inches in diameter, are white, red, pink, lavender, purple, and mixtures of these colors; in Hawai'i the blooming period is during the winter. Not known to seed in Hawai'i. Slow growth rate; easily transplanted.

GROWING CONDITIONS Quite adaptable, but grows best in cooler, more moist conditions; requires a very acid soil for optimum growth; may grow in almost pure humus, if that is well packed. Blooms best in sunny or partially shaded locations in cooler areas, and in partially shaded locations or morning-sun-only exposure in hot, dry Island areas.

USE Specimen plant; mass planting; low hedge; container plant; bonsai, colorful flowers.

PROPAGATION Grown from cuttings.

INSECTS/DISEASES For thrips, apply diazinon or malathion. For spider mites, use wettable sulfur.

PRUNING Will withstand severe pruning into formal, clipped forms, but will grow naturally into interesting irregular, mounded shapes. Pruning induces dense, compact growth.

FERTILIZING Apply acid fertilizer to the planting bed at 3-month intervals, and to container plants at monthly intervals. Water immediately, thoroughly after each application.

DISADVANTAGES Pests such as thrips and spider mites discolor foliage.

150

Theophrastaceae
(Theophrastus Family)

Theophrastus (370–285 B.C.), a student and close friend of Aristotle and now often referred to as the father of botany, was the eminent Greek naturalist and philosopher who wrote *Historia Plantarum*, a work that indicated the essential differences between the two great divisions of plants, the monocotyledons and the dicotyledons (all plants in this book are dicotyledons). The family Theophrastaceae includes 5 genera and about 110 species of tropical trees and shrubs, most of which are native to tropical America and the Caribbean area. Many members of this family exude pungent odors.

The genus *Jacquinia* seems to contain the plants in the family most often used in cultivation. **J. panamensis** is described in this book. Other interesting relatives include *Theophrasta americana*, an evergreen shrub with white flowers and apple-shaped fruits, which is native to Santo Domingo and Haiti; and *Clavija grandis*, a branchless shrub from Colombia, which produces leaves 3 feet long and clusters of orange flowers borne erect in a giant tuft at the tops of its stems.

Several *Jacquinia* species have been imported to Hawai'i, but as yet most of these are rather rare ornamental plants for Island gardens.

Jacquinia panamensis
Jacquinia

It is lovely to look at, but definitely not delightful to hold: this sturdy shrub is prepared to defend itself with needle-sharp spines at the tips of each stiff leaf. This species of *Jacquinia* is native to the Isthmus of Panama; 49 other members of the genus come from habitats spread across tropical America. One of them, *J. armillaris,* is called bracelet wood because its seeds are made into jewelry. Jacquinias probably are best known to the peoples of South America as sources of poisons and dyes. *J. armillaris* contains a highly toxic ingredient that Indians used in concocting a poison for their arrowheads; *J. barbasco* and several other species, including *J. umbellata* and *J. pungens,* bear fruits that, when crushed and spread by fishermen upon coastal waters, stupefy the quarry. *J. pungens* produces fragrant, long-lasting flowers that are strung into garlands; they also provide an important natural dye used in tropical America for coloring basketry plaited from palm leaves.

J. panamensis is something of a self-contained, live-and-let-live plant. It is hardy, resistant to most insects, diseases, drought or downpour, and to very salty conditions. In the garden its bright green crown is almost constantly bedecked with brilliant orange, long-lasting fruits. It is a superb container plant, requiring little care; both foliage and fruits are a source of vivid color.

The genus is named for Nicholas Joseph de Jacquin (1727–1817), professor of botany at Leyden, Holland; de Jacquin was a well-known collector and painter of West Indian flora; *panamensis* indicates the shrub's native home.

HABIT An erect, sprawling, or quite round, evergreen, woody shrub that grows to about 12 feet in height; has a single, large, dark brown trunk, with densely clustered interlacing branches growing thick to the ground. The most characteristic feature of the plant is its painfully spiny leaves; these are glossy, bright green, about 2 inches long; the foliage of several of these shrubs makes an impenetrable thicket. Small orange flowers are followed by orange ½-inch marble-like fruit. Slow growth rate; although difficult to move because of its spiny foliage, it can be transplanted.

GROWING CONDITIONS Adaptable; will grow anywhere in Hawai'i, even in the teeth of the salt wind at the beach, on dry slopes, or in the wettest valleys; it will grow in sun or shade, is very wind resistant, drought resistant, and will grow in almost any soil, even beach sand.

USE Specimen plant; mass planting; hedging; barrier planting; container plant.

PROPAGATION Grown from cuttings or seeds.

INSECTS/DISEASES For scale, apply malathion or summer oil.

PRUNING Withstands severe pruning, even to the ground; develops new sprouts readily; may be trimmed into informal natural hedges, or may be organized into treelike forms.

FERTILIZING Apply general garden fertilizer (10-30-10) to the planting bed at 6-month intervals, to container plants monthly. Water immediately and thoroughly each time.

DISADVANTAGES Because of painfully spiny leaf tips, this plant is difficult to cultivate or work around.

154

Myrsinaceae
(Myrsine Family)

Myrsine is the ancient Greek name for myrtle. However, the plants we know today as myrtles are members, not of the myrsine family, but of their own family, the Myrtaceae. The myrsine family includes 35 genera and about 1,000 species of tropical and subtropical trees and shrubs native mainly to South Africa and New Zealand. Toro *(Myrsine salicina)* is a New Zealand plant now grown ornamentally in Hawai'i. Another ornamental relative is a tropical American shrub, red mangrove *(Parathesis serrulata);* its common name notwithstanding, it is not related to the genuine members of the mangrove family (Rhizophoraceae).

A native Hawaiian *Myrsine*, kōlea *(M. lessertiana)*, is a handsome tree now grown ornamentally, but used formerly by Hawaiians as supporting timbers in their thatched houses. Kōlea wood also was fashioned into long, low anvils upon which the raw materials for making tapa were beaten into the finished sheets of the papery "fabric." The plant's red sap and charcoal were employed also as dyestuffs for designs painted or stamped upon the tapa.

Ardisia crispa
Hilo Holly, Manryō, Money Plant, Mata Puelandok

Hilo holly is neither a native of Hilo nor a holly. The plant is native to southern China, Japan, Malaysia, and Indonesia. It acquired its special Hawaiian name because it is so commonly grown in gardens of the Big Island's Hilo area and has escaped to grow wild there.

Japanese know the plant as manryō (ten-thousand yen plant or money plant) because of the great numbers of berries it bears. These are regarded as omens of good fortune. The plant is called mata puelandok in Malaysia. The Malays eat the small, red, somewhat sweet fruits. For medical purposes, the whole plant is crushed into an ointment for treating certain skin diseases; the juice of the fruits is considered a good earache remedy; the juice of the root is used as a tonic for fevers and intestinal complaints. A commercial medicine called sin-lo-san, derived from this plant, is sold in China for the treatment of sprains and broken bones.

Hilo holly, like the true hollies, develops clusters of brilliant red berries during the winter months; the leaves have somewhat the appearance of holly, but are soft and without spines. It is a small-scale, bonsai-like plant, commonly used in rock gardens and in formal Oriental gardens.

Ardisia, from *ardis*, meaning pointed, refers to the anthers of the flowers; *crispa*, meaning curly or uneven, describes the fluted leaf edges.

HABIT
An erect, evergreen, woody shrub that grows to about 8 feet in height; an irregular crown forms at the top of bare multiple stems. Foliage is dense, dark green, glossy; leaves have distinctive fluted edges. Clusters of small white flowers appear in the fall, followed by brilliant red, ¼-inch berries in the winter and spring; berries are grouped below the main foliage mass. Slow growth rate; easily transplanted.

GROWING CONDITIONS
Adaptable; prefers cool, moist areas, but will grow in drier locations if provided partial shade and roots are constantly moist; foliage turns yellow in strong sun.

USE
Specimen plant; mass planting; low hedge; container plant; attractive foliage and colorful berries.

PROPAGATION
Grows readily from seed. Offshoots with their roots may be removed carefully from the parent plant and set in well-drained potting soil until established.

INSECTS/DISEASES
For scale, apply malathion or summer oil. For mealybugs, use malathion.

PRUNING
Remove dead and damaged leaves and unsightly stalks. To reduce plant height, remove older stalks at ground level; this encourages lower vigorous new growth.

FERTILIZING
Apply general garden fertilizer (10-30-10) to the planting bed at 3-month intervals, and to container plants at monthly intervals. Water immediately and thoroughly in each case. In sandy or poor soils, plant is susceptible to deficiencies in minor elements (evidenced by yellowing foliage); use minor element fertilizers, either as foliar sprays or as soil applications, to correct this condition.

DISADVANTAGES
Highly susceptible to scale infestations and to minor element deficiencies.

158

Ardisia humilis
Duck's Eye, Mata Itek, Shoebutton

Who would ever know that a plant that looks like a flock of camouflaged ducks peering out of a leafy blind would have roots that persuade a balky elephant to eat? Malaysians do. Malay trainers serve the tonic roots of mata itek to the great pachyderms when they are off their feed. Duck's eye root, in tropical Asia, sometimes is administered to human patients suffering from stomachache, diarrhea, rheumatism, fever, and the aftereffects of childbirth. In the Philippines, *Ardisia* leaves are applied as poultices for wounds. Cooked flowers and fruits make flavorful condiments for Filipino fish dishes.

Duck's eye is native to Malaysia and Indonesia. Because it seeds so readily, new plants can rapidly cover open country. The shiny black-coated berries produce a good yellow dye that turns brown when used as ink on paper. Its hard, gray-hued wood is used sometimes in carpentry and woodworking. More often it is burned as a fuel.

Duck's eye is a highly colorful shrub with bright green, tidy foliage that when young is pink- or rose-toned. Perky pink flowers are followed by the brilliant red berries that turn to shiny black. Duck's eye has escaped from cultivation in the Hāna area on Maui, where it can be seen in thick stands along the roadsides. Larger than its better known cousin, **Hilo holly (*Ardisia crispa)*,** duck's eye grows into a tall informal hedge.

Ardisia, from *ardis,* meaning pointed, refers to the anther tips of the group's flowers; *humilis,* meaning humble, describes this species' small size compared with other ardisias. An English name for it is shoebutton.

HABIT An erect, evergreen, woody shrub that grows to about 12 feet in height; has multiple upright branches. Clean and glossy, oval, dark green mature leaves are about 3 inches long; new leaves are pink or bright rose. Clusters of small, pink, star-shaped flowers bloom at intervals throughout the year. The showy red, shiny, ¼-inch berries turn black as they ripen. Moderate growth rate; easily transplanted.

GROWING CONDITIONS Very adaptable; will grow in either very humid or very dry locations, in full sun or partial shade; will grow near the beach if protected from heavy salt winds.

USE Specimen plant; mass planting; informal hedges; container plant; colorful foliage, flowers, and berries.

PROPAGATION Grown from seed.

INSECTS/DISEASES For scale, apply malathion or summer oil.

PRUNING Prune to remove dead and damaged branches; plant is naturally compact, requires little pruning.

FERTILIZING Apply general garden fertilizer (10-30-10) to the planting bed at 3-month intervals, and to container plants at monthly intervals. Water immediately and thoroughly after each application.

DISADVANTAGES Plant reseeds itself prolifically in areas of high rainfall and so may become a pest.

Plumbaginaceae
(Leadwort Family)

Plumbago, meaning leadwort in Latin, is derived from *plumbum,* meaning lead. The ancients believed that certain kinds of plumbagos were beneficial in the treatment of lead poisoning. The family includes 19 genera and about 775 species of plants, generally perennial herbs and shrubs. Representatives of the family are native to most of the world's growing regions, but have evolved especially in coastal regions and salt plains.

Perhaps the plumbago most generally known is the many-named statice, or sea lavender, or everlasting flower *(Limonium latifolium),* so often used as a durable and colorful component in flower arrangements. Statice is native to Bulgaria and southern Russia. A relative from parts of northwest Europe called sea pink or thrift *(Armeria maritima)* is a well-known plant in temperate-zone rock gardens.

A wild plumbago native to the tropics of the Eastern Hemisphere, that has extended its range to Hawai'i, is hilie'e or 'ilie'e *(Plumbago zeylanica),* a poisonous plant used as a medicine both internally and externally.

Plumbago auriculata
Plumbago, Forget-me-not

The Xhosa and Zulu tribes of Africa attribute magical powers to *Plumbago auriculata.* These people believe that their medicine men can use plumbago root to confuse and confound an enemy, to chase away evil, and to ward off lightning. The root, when charred and powdered, is rubbed into incisions in the skin to provoke those intricate, raised, decorative welts so admired by tribesmen. Plumbago root is said to be an excellent styptic when applied as a powder, and a remedy for blackwater fever when taken in a liquid decoction. This last remedy must be considered to be drastic, for the root is very poisonous. The powdered root is used to remove warts in Africa and India. The Xhosas also inhale the powdered root as a kind of snuff to ease headaches. A native Hawaiian relative, hilie'e or 'ilie'e *(Plumbago zeylanica),* also poisonous, has a sap that was used by early Hawaiians to darken tattoos.

The name *Plumbago* comes from *plumbum,* meaning lead, because, according to Pliny, a preparation of plumbago was used by some Romans as a treatment for lead poisoning; *auriculata,* from *auricula* meaning ear, refers to the ear-lobe-shaped corolla. The name hilie'e is derived from the Hawaiian word *hili,* meaning bark for dyeing or a dark brown stain.

HABIT A sprawling, almost vinelike, evergreen, woody shrub that grows to about 15 feet in height; the thin, intertwining branch system is loose and straggly when allowed to grow unchecked, dense as a thicket when pruned to form. Small, bright green leaves are about 2 inches long; clusters of pale blue flowers appear constantly; individual flowers are tubes about ½ inch by 1½ inches, clustered densely into a dome about 3 to 4 inches in diameter. Insignificant seeds follow the blooms. Fast growth rate; easily transplanted. A white-flowered form is less common.

GROWING CONDITIONS Very adaptable; will grow nearly everywhere, even at the beach except in extreme salt conditions; grows and blooms best, and stays more compact, in full sun; will grow in nearly any kind of soil; requires constant ground moisture for optimum appearance, goes into a decline in drought conditions.

USE Mass planting; pruned hedge; colorful flowers.

PROPAGATION Almost always grown from cuttings.

INSECTS/DISEASES For scale, apply malathion or summer oil. For thrips and mealybugs, use diazinon or malathion. For Chinese rose beetles, to which plant is highly susceptible, apply one of the residual insecticides, such as carbaryl.

PRUNING Requires constant pruning to shape and to induce new growth and flowering; untrimmed plants become extremely leggy, climbing, and relatively flowerless; if allowed to grow unchecked, they will climb through and over other plants.

FERTILIZING Apply general garden fertilizer (10-30-10) at 4-month intervals. Water immediately.

DISADVANTAGES Requires more than the usual amount of pruning; subject to insect damage.

Oleaceae
(Olive Family)

The term Oleaceae comes from *olea,* a classical Latin name for the olive tree of commerce. Ever since man has cultivated the olive tree *(Olea europaea),* the olive branch has been a symbol of peace, prosperity, and good will. The family includes 29 genera and about 600 species from both temperate and tropical zones. In general the plants can be classified as either shrubs or trees.

Many relatives of the olive are known to ornamental horticulture. Among the most popular are forsythia *(Forsythia japonica),* a native of China; Indian jasmine *(Jasminum sambac),* called pīkake in Hawai'i, and its several close relatives; the fragrant Eastern European lilac *(Syringa vulgaris);* Chinese privet *(Ligustrum lucidum),* a well-known tree most often seen as a clipped hedge; Madagascar olive *(Noronhia emarginata),* a common beach tree in Hawai'i, and the white ash *(Fraxinus americana),* whose wood is commonly used in making implement handles. A Hawaiian relative, olopua *(Osmanthus sandwicensis),* is a tall evergreen tree used similarly by early Hawaiians for implement handles and for spears.

Osmanthus fragrans
Kwai-fah, Usugi-mokusei, Sweet Olive

This picturesque and fragrant plant is a native of the Himalayas, China, and Japan. Kwai-fah is one of the plant's Chinese names and the one most commonly used in Hawai'i. In Japan it is called usugi-mokusei. Kwai-fah is frequently seen growing around temples in the Orient. The plant's heady fragrance gives a characteristic aroma to the temple gardens. The flowers have a scent akin to that of apricots, and oftentimes are used in sachets. In China, kwai-fah is associated with legends about the moon, which are told and retold during the autumn lunar festivals when the plants are in flower. There too, the flowers are mixed among tea leaves, to scent them.

Kwai-fah is a plant of the warmer temperate regions. It grows best in Hawai'i's cooler, moist uplands, away from the hotter, drier plains. It is often grown as a potted specimen, placed on a cool, partially shaded lanai or terrace; the best location is near an open window through which the lovely perfume can enter the house. Indeed, the flowers are said to be among the most fragrant of all blossoms; one tiny flower can perfume an entire room.

Osmanthus, from *osme,* meaning smell, and *anthos,* meaning flower, refers to the plant's delightful fragrance; *fragrans,* meaning sweet-scented, emphasizes the meaning. English-speaking people sometimes refer to the plant as sweet olive.

HABIT An erect, woody, evergreen shrub that grows to about 15 feet in height; slender, picturesque stems show through a crown of sparse foliage composed of leathery, dull green leaves about 4 to 6 inches long. Tiny, apricot-scented, creamy-white flowers appear in small clusters at the bases of the leaves. The plant does not set fruit in Hawai'i. The species is protandrous; that is, an individual plant produces only male or only female flowers. Slow growth rate; easily transplanted.

GROWING CONDITIONS A poor plant for hot, dry areas; prefers cool, moist areas and well-watered, well-drained soil with high humus content; blooms well in sun or partial shade.

USE Specimen plant; container plant; fragrant flowers.

PROPAGATION Grown from woody cuttings.

INSECTS/DISEASES For scale, apply malathion or summer oil.

PRUNING May be pruned vigorously to induce heavy, sturdy foliage; however, extensive pruning will prevent flowering.

FERTILIZING Apply general garden fertilizer (10-30-10) to the planting bed at 3-month intervals, and to container plants at monthly intervals. Water immediately and thoroughly after each application. Kwai-fah foliage is almost always marred by browned leaf edges; this condition may be eliminated if fertilizer high in phosphorus and potassium (10-20-20) is applied periodically to the soil.

DISADVANTAGES Requires more than the usual amount of care; will not grow well in hot, dry locations.

Apocynaceae
(Periwinkle Family)

Apocynumis is the Greek name for certain of the periwinkle relatives. The word, stemming from *apo,* meaning away, and *kyon,* meaning dog, can be translated as dogbane, recalling the ages-old belief that many of the periwinkle relatives are poisonous to dogs. For this reason the group sometimes is called the dogbane family. The periwinkles include 180 genera and about 1,500 species, mostly tropical shrubs, twining shrubs, and vines. Several of the Apocynaceae yield useful substances, especially medicinal alkaloids.

Well-known relatives include an Arabian succulent, desert rose *(Adenium obesum);* a delicate vine, Confederate jasmine *(Trachelospermum jasminoides);* the highly fragrant Central American tree, lechoso *(Stemmadenia galeottiana);* two other Central American natives, common plumeria *(Plumeria acuminata)* and ''Singapore'' plumeria *(P. obtusa);* and the colorful Brazilian vine, allamanda *(Allamanda cathartica).* Equally well known relatives are the tropical American be-still tree *(Thevetia peruviana);* the tropical Pacific reva *(Cerbera manghas);* and the Easter lily vine *(Beaumontia grandiflora)* from India.

One of Hawai'i's best-loved plants is a periwinkle. Maile *(Alyxia olivaeformis),* a vine native to these islands, is twined into leis of heavenly fragrance that are given to people honored on very special occasions.

Allamanda oenotheraefolia
Bush Allamanda

Several species of allamandas, including the bush allamanda *(Allamanda oenotheraefolia),* are native to Brazil. In South America the sap of *A. violacea,* a vine with red-violet flowers, and the leaves of *A. cathartica,* a vine with yellow flowers, have poisonous properties, and, if administered in light doses, are useful as laxatives and in the treatment of colic. All three of these species thrive in Hawai'i's climate. Hawai'i's most common allamanda is *A. cathartica* var. *hendersonii,* a handsome, sturdy vine that has much larger deeper yellow flowers than does its parent.

Bush allamanda is quite similar in appearance to *A. cathartica* var. *hendersonii,* except that, as its name attests, it is very shrubby, and its flowers are about half the size of those of the vine. It produces attractive, identifying seedpods—large burrs—that are green at first, then gradually turn to brown, and rival the flowers in size. The colorful shrub is an attractive potted plant even when it is severely trained into a bonsai.

Allamanda is named for F. J. S. N. Allamand, eighteenth-century Dutch naturalist at the University of Leyden, a specialist in the flora of Brazil; he was a contemporary of Linnaeus, to whom he sent seeds of an *Allamanda* species; *oenotheraefolia,* from *Oenothera,* a group of plants collectively known as evening primroses, and *folium,* meaning a leaf, refers to the similarity of allamanda foliage to that of the evening primroses. The Greek word *oenothera* means wine-scenting (evening primrose roots, in ancient times, were employed in the flavoring of some wines).

HABIT An erect, woody, evergreen shrub that grows to about 8 feet in height and has many arching branches. Light green, pointed leaves are about 4 inches long. Bright yellow, trumpet-shaped flowers about 2 inches long and 2 inches in diameter appear constantly. Round, brown, burr-shaped fruit, about 2 inches in diameter, opens to expose many flat, russet seeds. Moderate growth rate; easily transplanted.

GROWING CONDITIONS Very adaptable; grows nearly anywhere at elevations under 1,000 feet, but is not a good beach plant; prefers sunny locations and rich, well-watered, well-drained soil.

USE Specimen plant; mass planting; container plant; bonsai plant; colorful flowers and unusual burrs.

PROPAGATION May be propagated by seeds or cuttings.

INSECTS/DISEASES For thrips, apply diazinon or malathion. For scale, use malathion or summer oil. For mealybugs, spray with malathion. For spider mites, apply wettable sulfur.

PRUNING May be vigorously pruned to shape or to remove dead or damaged wood; potted plants are adaptable to pruning procedures used in bonsai culture.

FERTILIZING Apply general garden fertilizer (10-30-10) to the planting bed at 4-month intervals, to container plants monthly. Water immediately and thoroughly each time.

DISADVANTAGES Susceptible to several pests.

Carissa macrocarpa
Natal Plum

About 30 species of *Carissa* have been found in Africa, Asia, and Australia. Natal plum, as its name implies, comes from South Africa. It is used as a source of food and as a natural barrier plant. The cranberry-flavored fruits, harvested when half ripe for making jellies and when ripe for pies, are commonly sold in Natal's markets. The plant's numerous, double-pronged thorns keep predators and trespassers away from hedged African gardens.

From *Carissa macrocarpa* horticulturists have developed many ornamental cultivars, including the groundcovers labelled 'Minima,' 'Horizontalis,' and 'Green Carpet'; the shrubs bred for special characteristics, such as the thornless 'Tomlinson,' 'Boxwood Beauty'; and the bonsai types, the large-fruited 'Fancy' and the dwarfish 'Tom Thumb.' Natal plums are noted for their almost perfect, glossy foliage, pure white, evening-fragrant flowers, and brilliant red, waxy fruits—all of which appear simultaneously.

Carissa is an aboriginal African name for the Natal plums; *macrocarpa* is from the Greek words *makros* (large) and *karpos* (fruit).

HABIT	Various plant forms, depending on horticultural cultivar, from foot-high, spreading groundcovers to shrubs over 20 feet in height. Double-pronged thorns protect tough branches and leaves. Glossy dark green foliage is evergreen. White, 3-inch, star-shaped flowers are fragrant at night. Brilliant red, edible, oval fruits form throughout the year. Moderate growth rate; easily transplanted.
GROWING CONDITIONS	Very adaptable; will grow almost anywhere, even in difficult situations; excellent beach plants; grow best in full sun, but will withstand some shade.
USE	Specimen plant; container plant; hanging baskets or window-box plant; hedge; living fence; small tree; groundcover (low-growing forms only); espalier.
PROPAGATION	An established horticultural cultivar must be reproduced from cuttings as seedlings revert to the original species. If seedlings are desired, remove seeds from fleshy covering and plant in well-drained potting soil.
INSECTS/DISEASES	For scale, apply malathion or summer oil. For thrips, use diazinon or malathion.
PRUNING	May be vigorously pruned to shape. Groundcover and small-leaved varieties often send out vigorous upright growth similar to that of the original species; if this growth is not consistently removed, the plants will revert to the parent type. Plants may be easily pruned into formal hedges, espalier or topiary forms, and as bonsai.
FERTILIZING	Apply general garden fertilizer (10-30-10) to the planting bed at 3-month intervals, and to container plants at monthly intervals. Water immediately and thoroughly in each case. In poor soils plant is susceptible to deficiencies in minor elements (evidenced by yellowing foliage); apply foliar sprays containing minor elements.
DISADVANTAGES	Some cultivars are very thorny. Constant pruning is required on most cultivars because thornless ones revert to thorny species; small-leaved cultivars revert to large-leaved species, and groundcover cultivars revert to the shrubby tree species.

Catharanthus roseus var. *ocellatus*
Madagascar Periwinkle, Kīhāpai, Chichirica

The Madagascar periwinkle, as this plant is called in Hawaiʻi, is a true periwinkle but not a native of Madagascar. Its original home was in Central America. The misnomer probably was applied in the early days of Western exploration, when sailing ships carried many plants from tropical America homeward. Subsequent naturalization in Madagascar led later collectors to believe that the plants were indigenous to that island.

This periwinkle is used in folk medicines of the Philippines, Malaysia, India, and South Africa as a treatment for diabetes. In parts of Africa it is considered a medicine for heart conditions. Leaves have been used for treating indigestion, as an emetic, and for wasp stings. In Madagascar the roots are used to treat toothache. Recently scientists have discovered components in the plant that show promise as inhibitors of certain animal tumors; present-day medical use includes chemical treatment of some forms of leukemia.

Catharanthus, from *katharus*, meaning pure or spotless, and *anthus*, meaning flower, describes the purity of the periwinkle blossoms; *roseus*, meaning rose-colored, refers to the original pink-flowered species; *ocellatus*, from *ocellus* meaning little eye, refers to the red center of each flower. Hawaiians call the plant kīhāpai, meaning garden, and Filipinos call it chichirica, rich milk, because of its fluid sap.

HABIT A bushy, herbaceous, evergreen shrub that grows to about 3 feet in height; stems are soft and weak. Glossy, dark green, oval leaves densely cover the plant. Flowers, about 2 inches in diameter, are white with a red center, and appear throughout the year. Pairs of inch-long seedpods follow; plants reseed themselves readily. Fast growth rate; easily transplanted when young.

GROWING CONDITIONS Very adaptable; while it prefers rich garden soils in full sun with constant ground moisture, it will grow under more adverse conditions, even at some beach sites.

USE Border and mass planting; container plant; hanging basket or window-box plant; constant colorful flowers.

PROPAGATION Seeds produce new flower colors. Cuttings must be used to maintain existing flower and leaf forms: cuttings from branch tips will root easily in water or in well-drained potting soil; cuttings will root best if leaves are not removed.

INSECTS/DISEASES For scale, apply malathion or summer oil. For thrips, use diazinon or malathion. For spider mites, spray with wettable sulfur.

PRUNING Prune back rangy plants to produce a more compact growth.

FERTILIZING Apply general garden fertilizer (10-30-10) to the planting bed at 3-month intervals, and to container plants at monthly intervals. In sandy or poor soils, plant is susceptible to deficiencies in minor elements (evidenced by yellowing foliage); use minor element fertilizers, either as foliar sprays or as soil applications.

DISADVANTAGES Relatively short-lived, lasting about 2 years.

Ervatamia divaricata

Crepe Gardenia, Firki Tagar, Rosebay, Ceylon Jasmine, Wax Flower, Tabernaemontana

The crepe gardenias are native to northern India, not to Ceylon as one of their vernacular names might imply. The single-flowered crepe gardenia *(Ervatamia divaricata)*, named firki tagar in Hindi and Bengali, is the parent of the double-flowered bara tagar *(E. divaricata* var. *flore-pleno)*, which Indians also call chandnee (moonbeam) because the white flowers seem to glow in the moonlight. English names for both flower forms, in addition to crepe gardenia and Ceylon jasmine, are rosebay, wax flower, and flower of love. The French, of course, call it fleur d'amour.

In India, especially in the lower Himalayan region, the seed pulp is used in making a strong red dye. The highly aromatic wood is burned as incense and its oil is an ingredient in perfumes. In folk medicine, various plant parts are used to treat high fevers, ulcers, eye diseases, and toothache. Indonesians take a decoction made from the roots to treat diarrhea. Indonesians and Malaysians make a cough medicine from the leaves. The foliage has been used for centuries in garlands and as table decorations; Indian women frequently wear the flowers in their hair, and on their garments as fastening devices.

Ervatamia, an old vernacular term for the plant, has replaced the melodious botanical epithet *Tabernaemontana* as the accepted generic name; *divaricata,* meaning spread apart, refers to the sparse branching habit.

HABIT An erect, woody, evergreen shrub that grows to about 15 feet in height; very nearly treelike, with a picturesque, branching habit. Glossy, dark green, pointed leaves are 5 to 6 inches long. Crisp, white, single or double, evening-fragrant, pinwheel flowers are 1 to 2 inches in diameter. Both leaves and flowers differ according to the several horticultural varieties. Pairs of brilliant orange fruits follow the blossoms, but rarely appear in Hawai'i. Moderate growth rate; easily transplanted.

GROWING CONDITIONS Very adaptable; will grow in cool or hot, moist or dry areas, but probably grows better in the hot, dry locations; thrives in full sun or partial shade.

USE Specimen plant; mass planting; container plant; small tree; constant flowers.

PROPAGATION In Hawai'i, new plants usually are propagated from cuttings and by airlayering.

INSECTS/DISEASES For scale, apply malathion or summer oil. For thrips and mealybugs, use diazinon or malathion. For oleander hawk moth caterpillars, apply one of the residual insecticides, such as carbaryl. For spider mites, spray with wettable sulfur.

PRUNING Prune to shape and to remove dead or damaged branches; may be drastically pruned to rejuvenate entire plant. Plants naturally require little pruning.

FERTILIZING Apply general garden fertilizer (10-30-10) to the planting bed at 3-month intervals, to container plants monthly. Susceptible to deficiencies in minor elements (browned leaf edges and deformed foliage); use minor element fertilizers.

DISADVANTAGES Minor element deficiencies and insect pests may be persistent problems.

Asclepiadaceae
(Milkweed Family)

The family Asclepiadaceae is named for Asklepios, Greek god of medicine, whom the Romans called Aesculapius. In Greek and Roman art, Asklepios was oftentimes shown in the company of Hygeia, goddess of wise living, and Panakeia, goddess of cure-alls (the English words *hygiene* and *panacea* derive from those names). Fittingly enough, several species of milkweeds are said to have medicinal value.

The milkweed family includes 130 genera and about 2,000 species, mostly tropical and subtropical shrubs, vines, and perennial herbs. The common milkweed *(Asclepia syriaca)* has long been used commercially: the silken seed-coverings are gathered for pillow-stuffing, and the stem fibers are spun into thread for cloth.

Ornamental relatives common to Hawaiian gardens are wax vine *(Hoya bicarinata)* from China and Australia; rosary vine *(Ceropegia woodii)*, India rubber vine *(Cryptostegia grandiflora)*, and carrion flower *(Stapelia nobilis)* from Africa; Madagascar jasmine *(Stephanotis floribunda)* from Madagascar; and Chinese violet *(Telosma cordata)*, known in Hawai'i as pakalana, from India and China.

Calotropis gigantea
Crown Flower, Mudar, Pua Kalaunu, Kapal-kapal, Giant Milkweed

In its native India the crown flower has religious, medicinal, and economic significance. Among Hindus the plant, called mudar, is sacred to the god Siva; it is a symbol, too, of one of the arrows of Kama, god of love. The plant contains a curious fluid known as mudarine that coagulates when warm but flows freely when cold. It is said to act like digitalis on the heart, and like ipecac on the bowels in cases of dysentery. Poisonous bites, leprosy, elephantiasis, worms, convulsions, epilepsy, spasmodic paralysis, toothache, earache, colds, asthma, and indigestion are other afflictions that have been treated with remedies derived from some part or another of the crown flower plant. The root is used to clean teeth. The bark produces a strong fiber for making textiles, fishnets, fishlines, and bowstrings. The seedpods yield a soft floss, similar to kapok, which is employed in weaving and in the stuffing of pillows and mattresses. A special kind of charcoal used in the production of gunpowder is derived from the wood. The sap contains sugars that can be fermented into an alchoholic beverage, and yields a tanning agent and dye.

The purple pua kalaunu was one of Queen Lili'uokalani's favorite blossoms. The white-flowered form was introduced to the Islands after the queen's death in 1917. The crownlike centers of the flowers are strung into long-lasting leis. In the Philippines rosaries are made of kapal-kapal flowers. In Southeast Asia the Chinese make candy of the flower centers.

Calotropis, from *kalos,* beautiful, and *tropis,* keel, describes a part of the flower; *gigantea* refers to the size of the plant.

HABIT An erect, evergreen, rounded shrub that grows to about 15 feet in height; forms an informal crown of long slender branches filled with milky sap. Leaves are large, gray-green, hairy. White or lavender crown-shaped flowers are 1½ inches long. Large oval seedpods, when mature, release numerous seeds, each equipped with a ''parachute'' and easily carried by the wind. Fast growth rate; easily transplanted.

GROWING CONDITIONS Very adaptable; prefers hot, dry locations, full sun.

USE Specimen plant; mass planting; hedge; colorful flowers; leis.

PROPAGATION Generally grown from cuttings, but seeds may be used as well.

INSECTS/DISEASES Larvae of the monarch butterfly feed exclusively on this plant in Hawai'i; may be controlled by applying the residual insecticide carbaryl.

PRUNING May be pruned severely to reduce plant size and to encourage bushiness; pruning induces vigorous new growth and flowering.

FERTILIZING Apply general garden fertilizer (10-30-10) to the planting bed at 3-month intervals.

DISADVANTAGES Contact with sap may irritate the skin of people who are sensitive. Monarch butterfly larvae can nearly destroy the foliage.

Verbenaceae
(Verbena Family)

Verbena is the Latin name for European vervain *(Verbena officinalis)*, used by Virgil and Pliny as a medicine. Several of the vervains were used by early physicians in treating defective vision. Seventy-five genera and about 3,000 species of herbs, shrubs, vines, and trees, most of them tropical or subtropical, make up this family.

A Hawaiian relative, pōhinahina or kolokolo kahakai *(Vitex ovata)*, an attractive plant with gray leaves and blue flowers, grows well along the Islands' beaches. Two Asian relatives often are grown in Hawaiian gardens—the small-flowered vitex *(V. parviflora)*, of some commercial value as a timber and reforestation tree; and the blue vitex *(V. trifolia* var. *subtrisecta)*, the gray-leaved bush commonly planted in hedges. Probably the most important commercial species is teak *(Tectona grandis)*, a tree native to India and Southern Asia that is highly prized for its beautifully grained, cinnamon-colored wood. Other useful relatives are fiddlewood *(Citharexylum spinosum)*, sandpaper vine *(Petrea volubilis)*, pink sandpaper vine *(Congea velutina)*, lippia *(Phyla nodiflora)*, and lemon verbena *(Aloysia triphylla)*.

Callicarpa americana
Beauty Bush, American Beautyberry, French Mulberry, Palis

Beauty bush is native to the southeastern United States where it is also known as American beautyberry and French mulberry. Although called French mulberry, this plant is completely unrelated to the true mulberries of the fig family (Moraceae) and is not a native of France; the misleading name is based on a resemblance between this plant and the edible mulberry *(Morus nigra)*. Filipinos call it palis (to sweep clean), a Tagalog name probably referring to the use of the branches as brooms. Sometimes in the Philippines, dried leaves of several *Callicarpa* species, including beauty bush, are smoked to relieve labored breathing; the green leaves are crushed and scattered upon water to stupefy fish. Malaysians employ these leaves in the same way to catch prawns—and also in treating people suffering from dropsy.

Beauty bush is a rather large, sprawling, open shrub. The berries are responsible for the plant's name: masses of violet berries cluster along its branches during the winter months, when few flowers are in bloom. A white-berried variety, *Callicarpa americana* var. *lactea,* sometimes seen in Hawai'i, is much more common on the mainland. The berried branches remain fresh for long periods after they have been cut, although the leaves will wilt almost immediately and must be removed from those portions used in flower arrangements.

Callicarpa, from *kallos,* meaning beauty, and *karpos,* meaning fruit, describes the handsome clusters of fruits; *americana* refers to the plant's native habitat; *lactea,* meaning milk, describes the variety's white fruits.

HABIT An erect, arching, woody, evergreen shrub that grows to about 10 feet in height and diameter; has a loose, flexible branching system and crown. Large, gray-green, pointed leaves, from 6 to 8 inches long are characteristically woolly on the undersides. Insignificant flowers are followed by clusters of brilliant pink to lavender to violet, ⅛-inch berries, the cluster at each joint being about 2 inches in diameter; berries appear usually from January to March. Moderate growth rate; easily transplanted.

GROWING CONDITIONS Grows best in the cool heights or wet valleys in Hawai'i; not a plant for hot, arid locations; requires rich, well-watered, well-drained soils; seems to thrive in airy, even windy, cooler regions; grows in either full sun or partial shade.

USE Specimen plant; mass planting; colorful berries.

PROPAGATION Grown from seed or cuttings.

INSECTS/DISEASES For Chinese rose beetles, apply one of the residual insecticides, such as carbaryl.

PRUNING Prune to remove dead or damaged wood; may be pruned heavily to induce new growth, flowering, and fruiting; weak stems and branches should be removed.

FERTILIZING Apply general garden fertilizer, high in phosphorus and potash, such as 10-20-20, at 4-month intervals. Water immediately and thoroughly after each application.

DISADVANTAGES May be damaged heavily by Chinese rose beetles in warmer, more humid areas.

Clerodendrum buchananii var. *fallax*
Pagoda Flower, Java Glorybower, Lau'awa

In Malaysia and Indonesia, the native habitat of this colorful shrub, clerodendrums are believed to have supernatural powers: to peoples of the region, the plants have *pepanggil,* the power to summon spirits. The flowers' gracefully protruding stamens are thought to have the power to beckon, and so hunters use the blossoms to lure game. Some clerodendrums are said to have *setawar* also, the power to provide protection from spirits, while others are *pakai panggil,* beautiful but evil-inducing. The native names for two species are translated as green witch's tongue (for *Clerodendrum serratum*) and nodding witch's tongue (for *C. deflexum*).

The pagoda flower is beneficial to the people of the region in perhaps more practical ways. Its crushed leaves are used in the treatment of dysentery, its root contains an antidote for certain snake bites, and a paste of the leaves is applied to infected burns. Javanese believe that pagoda flower, too, has *panggil-panggil,* magic powers. Newborn Amboinese infants are washed ceremonially in an infusion of its leaves.

Clerodendrum from *kleros,* meaning fate or chance, and *dendron,* meaning tree, the entire name meaning tree of fate, alludes to the clerodendrums' diverse qualities, some good, some harmful; *buchananii* honors Francis Buchanan-Hamilton (1762–1829), superintendent of the botanic garden at Calcutta; the reason for the variety name *fallax,* meaning false, is unclear. Hawaiians call the plant lau'awa, because its soft, velvety leaves resemble those of the 'awa *(Piper methysticum).* The name pagoda flower describes the plant's tiered inflorescences.

HABIT
An erect, woody, evergreen shrub that grows to about 8 feet in height; rather oval in general shape; branches long and sweep upward. Soft, velvety, heart-shaped, dark green leaves, about 6 to 8 inches in diameter, form a rather dense crown when shrub is well grown. Large, 12-by-15-inch clusters of brilliant scarlet flowers appear at ends of branches. Shiny black fruits and flowers may be present on the plant at the same time. Blooms almost continuously. Moderate growth rate; easily transplanted.

GROWING CONDITIONS
Very adaptable; will grow almost anywhere in Hawai'i except in extreme salt conditions; grows best in rich, well-watered, well-drained soil; requires constant moisture; tends to deteriorate if not cared for. Blooms in full sun or partial shade.

USE
Specimen plant; mass planting; colorful flowers; shiny black fruit.

PROPAGATION
Grown from seeds or cuttings.

INSECTS/DISEASES
For Chinese rose beetles, apply one of the residual insecticides, such as carbaryl.

PRUNING
May be pruned severely to induce new growth and flowering; weak stems and branches should be removed consistently.

FERTILIZING
Apply general garden fertilizer (10-30-10) to the planting bed at 4-month intervals.

DISADVANTAGES
Requires more than the usual amount of pruning to maintain compact appearance.

188

Clerodendrum nutans
Nodding Glorybower, Gan-yan-ta-po

This graceful shrub is native to northeastern India, Bangladesh, and Burma, where it is found growing at all elevations from sea level to about 3,000 feet. Burmese call the plant gan-yan-ta-po. *Clerodendrum nutans* was introduced to European horticulture in the nineteenth century, when an Englishman, M. R. Smith, sent seeds from northeastern Bengal to the botanic garden in Calcutta. Dr. Nathaniel Wallich (1786–1854), Danish-born superintendent of the garden, sent seeds from these first cultivated plants to Bretton Hall, an English college, in 1830. The plant is a relatively new introduction to Hawai'i, having been brought to the Islands from Western Samoa in 1969.

In its native home, nodding glorybower appears to be mainly ornamental in use, although many other species of clerodendrums have medicinal and preternatural associations. It is a tall, slender plant, growing in much the same form as does a panax. Its silhouette is delicate, slim, almost statuesque. The shrub has robust, dark green foliage which contrasts strikingly with the cascading, wisteria-like panicles of snow-white flowers. It is an excellent choice for small or narrow planting beds, and is also a fine container plant for a sunny terrace or a somewhat shaded lanai.

Clerodendrum, from *kleros,* meaning fate or chance, and *dendron,* meaning tree, the entire name meaning tree of fate, alludes to other species' diverse qualities, some of which act for good, others for harm; *nutans,* meaning nodding, refers to the delicate hanging flowers.

HABIT A very erect, tall, slender, evergreen shrub that grows to about 8 feet in height; the plant is cylindrical in form, having a single, bare, dark green stem with weeping branches and a light open crown; very different in appearance from most other plants because of this most graceful habit. Dark, glossy, slender, pointed leaves are about 6 inches long. Small clusters of brilliant white flowers hang from tips of branches during late fall to early spring. Occasional dark, shiny fruits, about ½ inch in diameter, follow the blossoms. Moderate growth rate; easily transplanted.

GROWING CONDITIONS Adaptable; will grow almost anywhere in Hawai'i except in extreme salt conditions; grows best in rich, well-watered, well-drained soil; requires constant moisture for optimum growth; blooms in full sun or partial shade.

USE Specimen plant; mass planting; handsome container plant; white flowers.

PROPAGATION Grown from seeds or cuttings.

INSECTS/DISEASES None of any consequence.

PRUNING May be pruned severely to induce new growth and flowering. For best results prune back in late spring, after the blooming period.

FERTILIZING Apply general garden fertilizer (10-30-10) to the planting bed at 4-month intervals, and to container plants at monthly intervals. Water immediately and thoroughly after each application.

DISADVANTAGES None.

190

Clerodendrum ugandense
Blue-flowered Clerodendrum

This *Clerodendrum,* a native of central East Africa, comes from a large plant genus. More than 400 *Clerodendrum* species are known, many of them native to Africa. As with Asian relatives, medicinal qualities are attributed also to many African species. Thus, a plant from Natal called wild violet and also usikisiki *(C. triphyllum* var. *ciliatum),* has roots and leaves that are used in the treatment of intestinal worms. Parts of several other species are employed in the dressing of wounds, treating skin ulcers and carbuncles, and in the relief of chest and stomach pains. Certain of the leaves are used as plasters for colic, rheumatism, and neuralgia.

C. ugandense is grown mainly for its ornamental value, for it is one of the world's very few plants that has truly blue flowers. At the beginning of the blooming season in the late fall, buds form in large upright clusters. The brilliant butterfly-shaped flowers open, a few at a time, beginning with the bottommost buds. Blue-flowered clerodendrum is a light, airy, sparsely foliaged shrub. During the warmer months, when its flowers do not appear, the plant tends to disappear visually into the background planting.

Clerodendrum, from *kleros,* meaning fate or chance, and *dendron,* meaning tree, the entire name meaning tree of fate, alludes to the clerodendrums' diverse qualities, some of which act for benefit, some for ill; *ugandense* refers to this species' native habitat, Uganda.

HABIT A very erect, tall, slender, evergreen shrub that grows to about 8 feet in height; it is oval in shape, having a single stem and erect, upright branches. A light open crown is formed by smooth, upright, olive-green, jagged-edged, and pointed leaves about 8 inches in length. Small clusters of two-toned blue flowers about 1 inch in diameter have distinctive arching stamens. From late fall to early spring, black, ½-inch berries follow the blossoms. Moderate growth rate; easily transplanted.

GROWING CONDITIONS Adaptable; will grow almost anywhere in Hawai'i except in extreme salt conditions; grows best in rich, well-watered, well-drained soil; requires constant moisture for optimum growth; blooms in full sun or partial shade.

USE Specimen plant; mass planting; sparse but colorful flowers.

PROPAGATION Grown from seeds or cuttings.

INSECTS/DISEASES None of any consequence.

PRUNING May be pruned severely to induce new growth and flowering. For best results prune back in late spring, after the blooming period.

FERTILIZING Apply general garden fertilizer (10-30-10) to the planting bed at 4-month intervals. Water immediately and thoroughly after each application.

DISADVANTAGES None.

Duranta repens

Golden Dewdrop, Espina Blanca, Espina Negro, Violetina, Velo de Novia, Velo de Viuda, Adonis, Garbancillo, No-me-olvides, Sky Flower

Golden dewdrop, a native of the Caribbean islands and of Central and South America, is a plant with many names. Mexicans know the white-flowered variety as velo de novia (bride's veil) or espina blanca (white thorn), and the purple-flowered variety as velo de viuda (widow's veil) or espina negro (black thorn). In Cuba it is violetina (little violet) or no-me-olvides (forget-me-not). In Colombia the plant is called garbancillo (little garbanzo).

Golden dewdrop is one of the most common hedge plants in tropical and subtropical countries. Although some varieties are thornless, others are spiny-stemmed and are most often used as barrier plants and for lining cattle fences. The plant is quite poisonous because it contains considerable amounts of hydrocyanic acid. The poisonous berries are used in the treatment of fevers and intestinal worms. The flowers are said to have stimulant properties. In India mosquito repellant is made from the berries; another preparation from the macerated fruit is said to kill mosquito larvae.

Golden dewdrop is an excellent plant for ornamental hedges and backgrounds. Often it is pruned into a handsome multiple- or single-stemmed tree. Several varieties of *Duranta* grow in Hawai'i, including the thorny and thornless, the white-flowered and blue-flowered, and a form with variegated foliage. Bonsai trainers have grown extremely attractive specimens of each.

Duranta is named for Castor Durantes, sixteenth-century Roman physician; *repens*, creeping, refers to the pendent habit of flowers and fruits.

HABIT   An erect, woody, evergreen shrub that grows to about 18 feet in height and is almost treelike when mature. Many spreading branches are covered with dark green foliage; one variety has green and white foliage. Blue or white flowers hang in clusters. Clusters of golden fruits appear at intervals. Moderate growth rate; easily transplanted.

GROWING CONDITIONS   Very adaptable; equally at home in moist or dry areas, full sun or partial shade.

USE   Specimen plant; small tree; mass planting; informal hedge; container plant; colorful foliage, flowers, and fruit.

PROPAGATION   Grown easily from seeds or cuttings. Form with green and white leaves must be propagated from cuttings.

INSECTS/DISEASES   For scale, apply malathion or summer oil. For grasshoppers, spray with carbaryl. For thrips, mealybugs, and southern green stinkbugs, use diazinon or malathion. Several stinkbug parasites and predators help to control this pest.

PRUNING   Prune to remove dead and damaged branches and to shape; may be pruned vigorously to induce new growth and flowering; may be shaped into bonsai.

FERTILIZING   Apply general garden fertilizer (10-30-10) to the planting bed at 2-month intervals, and to container plants at monthly intervals. Water immediately and thoroughly.

DISADVANTAGES   Susceptible to several insect pests.

Holmskioldia sanguinea
Cup-and-Saucer Plant, Cups and Saucers, Chinese Hat Plant

The cup-and-saucer plant is native to the foothills of the Indian Himalayas, where it grows at elevations of from 3,000 to 5,000 feet. Of the several cup-and-saucer plants included in the genus *Holmskioldia,* most are primarily ornamental plants. The plants are distinctive because of their unusual flowers: whereas the corollas of most flowers are composed of several petals, those of the holmskioldias are simply a single funnel-shaped tube. And whereas the calyxes, or basal portions, of most flowers are green and leaflike, those of the holmskioldias are single, petal-like, and saucer-shaped.

H. sanguinea, with its russet flowers, is the most common ornamental cup-and-saucer plant. A form of the species, *H. sanguinea* f. *citrina,* has citron-yellow flowers. All the common names that have been given to these plants refer to the distinctive shapes of their flowers.

Cup-and-saucer plants are large, loose, open shrubs, almost constantly in bloom. The plants tend to a sprawling ranginess, but with vigorous and constant pruning, they may be trained into an almost unlimited variety of shapes, including topiary shrubs and formal hedges. Blossoms appear throughout much of the year, even when the plant is kept severely pruned.

Holmskioldia is named for Theodor Holmskiold (1732–1794), Danish nobleman and botanist; *sanguinea,* blood, refers to the brick-red flowers; *citrina,* citron, describes that form's lemon-yellow blossoms.

HABIT An erect, woody, evergreen shrub that grows to about 10 feet in height in an airy, open crown of multiple stems and arching branches. Dark green, hairy leaves are about 2 to 3 inches long. Clusters of salmon-colored flowers of a definite cup-and-saucer shape appear on and off throughout the year, but the shrub tends to bloom most fully from September through November. Not known to seed in Hawai'i. Moderate growth rate; easily transplanted.

GROWING CONDITIONS Highly adaptable; will grow almost anywhere except in extreme salt conditions; prefers cool, moist areas and full sun.

USE Specimen plant; mass planting; pruned or unpruned hedge; container plant; colorful flowers.

PROPAGATION Grown from cuttings.

INSECTS/DISEASES For scale, apply malathion or summer oil. For thrips and mealybugs, use diazinon or malathion.

PRUNING May be pruned severely to shape and to induce new growth and flowering.

FERTILIZING Apply general garden fertilizer (10-30-10) to the planting bed at 3-month intervals, and to container plants at monthly intervals. Water immediately and thoroughly after each application. In sandy or poor soils, plant is susceptible to deficiencies in minor elements (evidenced by yellowing foliage); use minor element fertilizers, either as foliar sprays or as soil applications, to correct this condition.

DISADVANTAGES Will become rangy without constant pruning.

Holmskioldia tettensis
Lavender Cup-and-Saucer Plant, Cups and Saucers

Holmskioldia tettensis is an African relative of the better-known Indian species, **H. sanguinea.** It is native to the region of the Shire and lower Zambezi rivers of southeast Africa. Eleven other species are native to Africa, Madagascar, and India to Malaysia. Holmskioldias generally are thought of as ornamental plants. This particular species is highly regarded because of its numerous mauve-lavender cup-and-saucer flowers. The cup appears first as a tiny star-shaped bud in the center of the larger saucer-like calyx, but soon after the cup-shaped corolla has formed, it falls from the plant, leaving the empty saucers to provide generous spots of color in the garden.

Like other holmskioldias, this shrub is tall, loose-growing, and open in habit. It resists attempts to train it by pruning into a more compact mass. Pruning to accentuate its tall, linear, open qualities is far more successful. The plant is an excellent one for espaliering against trellises and walls, or for training into single- or multiple-stemmed standards. Although it blooms prodigiously for much of the year, bringing high color into the garden, the shrub is somewhat nondescript in its off-blooming periods.

Holmskioldia is named for Theodor Holmskiold (1732–1794), a Danish botanist; *tettensis* is named for the African village of Tete on the Zambezi River, where the plant was first collected for European horticulture.

HABIT
An erect, woody, evergreen shrub that grows to about 15 feet in height in an airy, open crown of multiple stems and arching branches. Dark green, rounded, 3-inch leaves have toothed edges. Clusters of mauve flowers have the familiar cup-and-saucer configuration; tends to bloom most fully from September through November, although it will bloom irregularly throughout the year. Not known to set seed in Hawai'i. Moderate growth rate; easily transplanted.

GROWING CONDITIONS
Highly adaptable; will grow almost anywhere except in extreme beach conditions; grows equally well in hot dry areas and in rain-forest conditions. Blooms best in full sunny locations.

USE
Specimen plant; mass planting; severely pruned hedge; colorful flowers.

PROPAGATION
Grown from cuttings.

INSECTS/DISEASES
For scale, apply malathion or summer oil. For thrips and mealybugs, use diazinon or malathion.

PRUNING
May be pruned severely to shape and to induce new growth and flowering; heavy pruning required to produce thick growth. Best pruned in the winter, directly after the main flowering period.

FERTILIZING
Apply general garden fertilizer (10-30-10) to the planting bed at 3-month intervals. Water immediately and thoroughly after each application. In sandy or poor soils plant is susceptible to deficiencies in minor elements (evidenced by yellowing foliage); use minor element fertilizers, either as foliar sprays or as soil applications.

DISADVANTAGES
Will become rangy and straggly without constant pruning.

Lantana camara
Lantana, Cinco Negritos, Comida de Paloma, Lākana

Lantana is a very common roadside plant in its native Mexico. In Sinaloa State the shrub provides a favorite remedy for snakebite; a strong decoction of the leaves is taken internally and a poultice of leaves is applied to the snakebite itself. Moreover, the cooked leaves are eaten as a remedy for stomachaches and are applied as a kind of liniment for rheumatism. Mexicans call the plant cinco negritos (five little black ones) because its small, shiny, black fruits appear in clusters of five. It is also called comida de paloma (pigeons' food) because of the birds' liking for the berries. Malaysians and Indonesians use the plants in ways similar to those of Mexicans: as a poultice for wounds and skin ulcers, and as a liniment for rheumatism.

Lantana is an old name once applied to one of the viburnums, an unrelated group of plants in the honeysuckle family (Caprifoliaceae); *camara*, meaning a simple carpel, describes the flower part out of which the fruit develops. Hawaiians call the plant lākana, a phonetic transliteration of its common English name. Another Hawaiian name is mikinolia hihiu, which means wild magnolia, but why it should be called a magnolia is unclear.

HABIT An erect, woody, evergreen shrub that grows to about 15 feet in height and forms an irregular crown of thorny, multiple branches. Hairy, aromatic, dark green leaves are about 1 to 5 inches long. Flower clusters, 2 inches in diameter, are composed of purple, pink, orange, yellow, or white florets or mixtures of these colors. Blooms continually throughout the year. Berry-like black fruits follow the flowers. Fast growth rate; easily transplanted.

GROWING CONDITIONS Very adaptable; will grow almost anywhere, but prefers the hot, dry, sunny lowland areas if provided with periodic irrigation.

USE Specimen plant; mass planting; low hedge or border; container plant; colorful flowers. A dwarf cultivar is now most commonly grown.

PROPAGATION Named horticultural cultivars are always propagated from cuttings; new varieties are produced from seed.

INSECTS/DISEASES Lantana can be an annoying weed because it has escaped from cultivation in Hawai'i and invaded farmlands; as a result, several insect enemies have been introduced to destroy the wild growth. These insects may kill domesticated lantana plantings. Control by spraying with malathion at least 2 times, 14 days apart. Repeat as needed.

PRUNING May be pruned vigorously to shape and to induce new growth and flowering.

FERTILIZING Apply general garden fertilizer (10-30-10) to the planting bed at 4-month intervals, and to container plants at monthly intervals. Water immediately and thoroughly after each application. In sandy or poor soils plant is susceptible to deficiencies in minor elements (evidenced by yellowing foliage); use minor element fertilizers, either as foliar sprays or as soil applications, to correct this condition.

DISADVANTAGES Spreads rapidly, may become a neighborhood weed; subject to insect attack.

200

Solanaceae
(Tomato Family)

The tomato family, sometimes also called the nightshade family, takes its Latin name from *Solanum,* an old term for several of the plants now classified within this group. The family consists of 90 genera and about 2,000 species, most of which are native to the temperate and tropical regions of Central and South America. These include some of the world's most important food crops: tomato *(Lycopersicon esculentum),* potato *(Solanum tuberosum),* chili pepper *(Capsicum annuum),* bell pepper *(C. annuum* var. *grossum)*—all natives of tropical America—and eggplant *(S. melongena),* a native of Southeast Asia.

The ancients attributed medicinal and even supernatural properties to many plants in the tomato family. Probably the best known of these in legend is mandrake *(Mandragora officinarum),* a native of Europe and Africa; because of the suggestive shapes its roots can assume, it has played an important role in human imagination as a sex symbol and as an object of power in witchcraft. The so-called deadly nightshades, the family's most poisonous members, include the important medicinal herb belladonna *(Atropa belladonna),* from which the antispasmodic atropine is obtained, and Jimson weed *(Datura stramonium),* from which stramonium, a medicine for treating asthma, is derived. Tobacco *(Nicotiana tabacum)* probably is the family's most important and increasingly controversial nonfood crop.

Ornamental relatives include cup of gold *(Solandra hartwegii),* petunia *(Petunia × hybrida),* and salpiglossis *(Salpiglossis sinuata).* A Hawaiian native, 'ae'ae *(Lycium sandwicense),* is a small shrub found growing in beach areas and other salt-rich locations.

Brunfelsia americana
Lady-of-the-Night, Dama de Noche

The brunfelsias add great ornamental value to a family otherwise prized for its wealth of vegetables. The sun-loving *Brunfelsia americana,* a native of the Caribbean, has flowers that are milk-white when they open, then deepen to creamy yellow. These flowers exude a heady fragrance from dusk to dawn, a quality that has inspired its vernacular name, dama de noche (lady of the night). A variety, *B. americana* var. *pubescens,* has downy leaves and produces more flowers than does its parent.

In Martinique, the astringent fruits of lady-of-the-night are processed into a medicine for treating intestinal complaints, specifically chronic diarrhea. Plant parts of a close relative, Manaca raintree *(B. hopeana),* are used in tropical America in the treatment of rheumatism; they contain a highly dangerous substance, menacine, which is similar to strychnine in its effects on the body.

A tall, vase-shaped plant, lady-of-the-night is well used either as a specimen shrub or as material for an informal hedge. The fragrance-sensitive gardener should be warned that the scent from the blossoms may be too pervasive for some people to endure. It is a semidesert, hot-weather plant, and thrives on Hawai'i's dry, leeward slopes where annual rainfall is measured at 10 inches or less per year.

Brunfelsia is named for Otto Brunfels (1489–1534), of Mentz, a Carthusian monk and physician, who published in 1530 the first accurate European botanical illustrations; *americana* refers to the plant's native habitat.

HABIT An erect, woody, evergreen shrub that grows to about 8 feet in height; its dense crown is an oval, upright form. Glossy, yellow-green, rounded leaves are about 2 to 3 inches in diameter. Blooms in the spring, producing masses of trumpet-shaped, 2-inch flowers that are lightly fragrant during the day, very fragrant at night. Round, orange-colored, ½-inch berries may appear on the plant at the same time with flowers. Moderate growth rate; easily transplanted.

GROWING CONDITIONS Adaptable; will grow almost anywhere in Hawai'i except in salt-exposed areas; prefers hot, dry, sunny locations with rich, well-watered, well-drained soil. Not a beach plant.

USE Specimen plant; mass planting; container plant; fragrant, colorful flowers.

PROPAGATION Grown from seeds or cuttings.

INSECTS/DISEASES For grasshoppers, apply diazinon.

PRUNING Does not take particularly well to pruning; prune lightly only to shape.

FERTILIZING Apply general garden fertilizer (10-30-10) to the planting bed at 4-month intervals, and to container plants at monthly intervals. Water immediately and thoroughly after each application.

DISADVANTAGES Fragrance may be too strong for some.

Brunfelsia latifolia
Yesterday-Today-and-Tomorrow, Kiss-Me-Quick

The shade-loving *Brunfelsia latifolia,* from tropical America, has flowers that are blue-violet when they open, then fade to lavender, and finally to white on succeeding days. The several variations in color appear on a plant at the same time, and because of the flowers' changeable appearance, fanciful gardeners have given the plant such descriptive appellations as yesterday-today-and-tomorrow, and kiss-me-quick (before-I-fade). It is one of the relatively few plants that have blue, or almost blue, flowers. Having little medicinal or economic value, it is grown primarily for its beauty.

Yesterday-today-and-tomorrow brings color to the tropical garden during the late winter months when few other plants are in bloom. It is a harbinger of spring with its bright, cheerful presence and crisp spots of brilliant color. Its flowers release a delightful fragrance both by day and by night. One of the shrub's most prized characteristics is its ability to bloom well even in shady areas; it blooms brightly in darkened garden areas where most other flowering plants will produce only foliage.

Brunfelsia is named for Otto Brunfels (1489–1534) of Mentz, a Carthusian monk and physician, who published in 1530 the first accurate European botanical illustrations; *latifolia,* from *latus,* meaning broad or wide, and *folium,* meaning a leaf, describes this species' relatively broad leaves.

HABIT A spreading, woody, evergreen shrub that grows to about 8 feet in height in a loose crown of irregular branches. Dark green, glossy, rounded leaves are 2 to 3 inches in diameter. Blooms from late winter to early summer; flowers, each about 1 inch in diameter, open a violet color, then fade to white. Small, orange, single, ½-inch berries sometimes follow the bloom. Moderate growth rate; easily transplanted.

GROWING CONDITIONS Adaptable, but prefers cool, moist areas and filtered sunlight; requires protection from strong winds and full sun; not a beach plant; requires rich, well-drained, well-watered soil.

USE Specimen plant; mass planting; container plant; flower color and fragrance.

PROPAGATION Grown from seeds or cuttings.

INSECTS/DISEASES For scale, apply malathion or summer oil. For thrips, use diazinon or malathion.

PRUNING May be drastically pruned to desired form or to reduce size; plant is naturally loose-growing, should not be maintained as a topiary form; pruning after flowering induces new growth and vigorous blooming during the following season.

FERTILIZING Apply general garden fertilizer (10-30-10) to the planting bed at 3-month intervals, and to container plants at monthly intervals. Water immediately and thoroughly after each application. In sandy or poor soils, plant is susceptible to deficiencies in minor elements (evidenced by yellowing foliage); use minor element fertilizers, either as sprays or as soil applications, to correct this condition.

DISADVANTAGES Will not grow well in areas of extreme exposure.

206

Cestrum nocturnum
Night Cestrum, Reina de la Noche, Galan de Noche,
Hierba Hedionda, Night-blooming Jasmine, 'Ala Aumoe

This native of the Caribbean and Central American regions is a plant of many names. Among the most common are reina de la noche (queen-of-the-night), also a name for **Datura candida;** galan de noche (night elegance); and hierba hedionda (offensive herb). As these several names reveal, the plants' pervasive aroma evokes diverse reactions. Most people find it sweetly sensuous; other dislike it.

Leaves and fruits of the shrub are listed in the Mexican pharmacopoeia as being acceptable remedies in the treatment of epilepsy and certain other disorders. Sometimes parts of the plant play a role in magic. The leaves and fruits are toxic to livestock.

Night cestrum is not an especially handsome plant. Generally it is considered as background material, placed in the garden more to be sensed than seen in Hawai'i's warm evenings. It is closely related to day cestrum *(Cestrum diurnum)*, whose scented flowers open during the morning hours. Night cestrum has escaped from cultivation in Hawai'i and is naturalized in a number of the wet valleys, where its seeds germinate readily.

Cestrum, from *kestron,* meaning spike, is a name the Greeks applied to several different species of plants; *nocturnum* (belonging to the night) and *diurnum* (belonging to the day) describe the blooming characteristics of the two species. Hawaiians call the night bloomer 'ala aumoe (fragrant at night). Two other Hawaiian names are kūpaoa (strong odor), and onaona Iāpana, meaning soft fragrance from Japan—that is, from far away, referring to the fact that one can smell the blossoms from a great distance.

HABIT   An erect, woody, evergreen shrub that grows to about 10 feet in height in a loose, oval crown. Leaves are glossy, light green. Hanging clusters of thin, pale yellow, trumpet-shaped flowers, 1 inch long, bloom on and off throughout the year, are fragrant only at night. Small white berries follow. Plant reseeds itself readily. Fast growth rate; easily transplanted.

GROWING CONDITIONS   Very adaptable; will grow readily almost anywhere except in strong salt winds and exposed beach areas.

USE   Background plant grown primarily for nocturnal fragrance.

PROPAGATION   Cuttings will root easily; may also be grown from seed.

INSECTS/DISEASES   For scale, apply malathion or summer oil. For thrips, use diazinon or malathion. For spider mites, spray with wettable sulfur.

PRUNING   Should be pruned back to about 3 feet from the ground after flowering to assure more vigorous, more attractive plant with optimum bloom the following season.

FERTILIZING   Apply general garden fertilizer (10-30-10) to the planting bed at 3-month intervals; fertilize heavily after drastic pruning. Water immediately and thoroughly each time.

DISADVANTAGES   Plant becomes rangy without vigorous pruning; fragrance may be too strong for some.

Datura candida
Angel's Trumpet, Trompeta, Campana, Campanilla Blanca,
Reina de la Noche, Nānā Honua

These beautiful flowers are heavenly to see, but for those who use this plant unwisely, angel's trumpet may well sound the death knell. The leaves are extremely poisonous; unconsciousness, delirium, and death can result from ingestion of any part of the plant. For centuries, in its native South American region, from Chile northward to Colombia, tribal medicine men have used the plants in treating sicknesses, in mystic rituals, and magical ceremonies. In Costa Rica the flowers are sometimes placed near pillows to help induce sleep. The leaves, when properly prepared, are applied as a poultice and pain reliever for external sores and broken bones. A preparation of angel's trumpet sometimes is substituted for belladonna *(Atropa belladonna)*, a close relative, in the treatment of pain and in dilating the pupils of the eyes. European horticulture and medicine became aware of the plant after its introduction to the court of Philip II of Spain in the sixteenth century.

Angel's trumpet is a plant of many names, several of which are Spanish in origin: trompeta (trumpet), campana (bell), campanilla blanca (little white bell), and reina de la noche (queen of the night), also a name for **Cestrum nocturnum,** are only a few. Hawaiians, thinking of the pendent flowers as looking toward the earth, call it nānā honua (earth-gazing).

Datura comes from the Hindu word *dhatura,* itself probably derived from an Arabic name (tatoral) for a close relative, the thorn apple *(Datura stramonium); candida,* shining white, refers to the luminous white flowers.

HABIT	An erect, woody, evergreen, almost treelike shrub that grows to about 20 feet in height; single trunk and spreading branches form a round-headed, open crown. Leaves are large, soft, fuzzy, about 15 inches in diameter. Pure white or salmon, fragrant, bell-shaped flowers are about 12 inches long and appear at intervals throughout the year; flowers are especially fragrant at night. Not known to fruit in Hawai'i. Moderate growth rate.
GROWING CONDITIONS	Prefers the cool valleys and ridges; requires rich, well-watered, well-drained soil.
USE	Specimen plant; mass planting; untrimmed hedges; fragrant white flowers.
PROPAGATION	Can be transplanted, but usual method is to start new plants from cuttings.
INSECTS/DISEASES	For Chinese rose beetles, apply one of the residual insecticides, such as carbaryl. For grasshoppers, use diazinon. For spider mites, spray with wettable sulfur.
PRUNING	May be pruned extensively to reduce height and to induce new growth and flowering.
FERTILIZING	Apply general garden fertilizer (10-30-10) to the planting bed at 4-month intervals.
DISADVANTAGES	Does not withstand dry conditions, nor grow well in windy locations. Sap may be irritating to some people. All parts are poisonous.

Scrophulariaceae
(Snapdragon Family)

Scrofula, a form of tuberculosis affecting the lymph glands of the neck, was treated in Medieval Europe with a variety of medicines, some of which were derived from certain species of plants now included in this family. Members of the snapdragon family sometimes are referred to as figworts, because of the fig-shaped nodules that develop naturally on stems and roots of certain species. The family is a large one, numbering 220 genera and about 3,000 species, most of which are herbs and low shrubs. A number of species are parasitic, attaching themselves, in many cases, to the roots of grasses. Commercially important relatives are foxglove *(Digitalis purpurea)*, source of the heart stimulant and diuretic; musk *(Mimulus moschatus)*, an ingredient of perfumes; and kiri *(Paulownia tomentosa)*, a prized timber tree in its native Japan. Another relative, *Schweinfurthia sphaerocarpa*, sometimes is used in the treatment of typhoid fever in India. There also, powdered parts of this plant are inhaled like snuff in treating nosebleed.

Colorful flowering relatives often grown in gardens are calceolaria (*Calceolaria* spp.), snapdragon *(Antirrhinum majus)*, veronica *(Veronica arvensis)*, and beard-tongue *(Penstemon cobaea)*.

Angelonia salicariaefolia
Angelonia, Angelon

Angelonia is a shrub native to tropical America. In some parts of Venezuela it is used as a medicine to induce perspiration in fevered patients. Essentially an ornamental plant, angelonia is seen frequently in gardens and along roadsides in Central and South America.

Angelonia is a herbaceous perennial shrub, quite weak and tender in structure. The beauty of the shrub is in its blossoms. The flowers of one form are pure white, of another, pink, of still another, lavender, while a fourth bears the variegated purple and white blooms shown in the accompanying illustration. It is a somewhat unusual plant in Hawai'i, being grown mainly as an ornamental curiosity.

The generic name is derived from the common Spanish term for the plant, angelon (angelic figure), possibly referring to the "heavenly" scent of the leaves when they are broken or rubbed; *salicariaefolia*, from *salicaria* meaning willow-like, and *folium*, meaning leaf, describes the slender leaves, resembling those of some willows.

HABIT A herbaceous, shrubby, evergreen perennial that grows to about 3 feet in height; semiwoody, multiple stems grow from the base. Slender leaves are about 3 inches long. Erect, foot-long flower spikes bloom at intervals throughout the year; cuplike flowers are lavender, white, lavender and white, or rose-pink. Insignificant brown seedpods follow the bloom. Moderate growth rate; easily transplanted.

GROWING CONDITIONS Very adaptable; will grow nearly anywhere in Hawai'i except in extreme beach conditions; prefers cool, sunny locations, plentiful ground moisture.

USE Specimen plant; mass plantings; container plant; colorful flowers.

PROPAGATION May be grown from seed, but is almost always grown from cuttings.

INSECTS/DISEASES For thrips, apply diazinon or malathion.

PRUNING Plant may be pruned severely to produce compact, vigorous growth and flowering.

FERTILIZING Apply general garden fertilizer (10-30-10) to the planting bed at 4-month intervals, and to container plants at monthly intervals. Water immediately and thoroughly after each application.

DISADVANTAGES Plant may become rangy without periodic pruning.

Russelia equisetiformis

Coral Plant, Lluvia de Coral, Lluvia de Fuego, Arete de la Cocinera, Fountain Plant, Firecracker Plant, Lōkālia

Coral plant, a purely ornamental native of Mexico, is known as lluvia de coral (rain of coral) and lluvia de fuego (rain of fire) in Central America. Possibly the most descriptive Spanish name is arete de la cocinera (cook's earrings). This colorful shrub, much like **ribbon bush *(Homalocladium platycladum)*,** has virtually no foliage. Its reedlike stems do most of the photosynthesis necessary to sustain the plant. The true leaves are small, scaly bracts that protrude from the stems at the base of the flower clusters.

One of the most colorful of Hawai'i's shrubs, coral plant is almost constantly ablaze with flowers. It is a delicate, succulent plant, with slender, wispy branches spilling out like fountaining water. It is best used where cascading forms are desired, or as a groundcover on an embankment or thrusting out from a rocky cliff or ledge. The shrub is handsomely displayed when it is grown at the top of a retaining wall or in a high planter box from which it can fall gracefully over the edge. It is an excellent plant for a hanging basket, and will grow and bloom beautifully in full sunny conditions.

Russelia is named for Alexander Russel (d. 1768), Englishman and author of the work *Natural History of Aleppo; equisetiformis,* from *equestris* (pertaining to the horse), and *forma,* meaning form or shape, refers to the horsetail appearance of the branches. Other English names are fountain plant and firecracker plant (sometimes causing confusion with the firecracker vine, *Pyrostegia venusta*). Hawaiians call the shrub lōkālia, their soft-spoken version of *Russelia.*

HABIT	A sprawling, herbaceous, evergreen shrub that grows to about 6 feet in height; has a dense, arching crown composed of many weeping green branches, sparsely covered by small, bright green, insignificant leaves. Long clusters of coral-red, tubular, inch-long flowers hang at the branch tips, appearing throughout the year. Does not fruit in Hawai'i. Moderate growth rate; easily transplanted.
GROWING CONDITIONS	Very adaptable; will grow almost anywhere except in extreme salt conditions. Requires rich, well-watered, well-drained soil; flowers best in full sun.
USE	Specimen plant; mass planting; container plant; hanging basket; embankment plant; colorful flowers.
PROPAGATION	Very easily grown from cuttings.
INSECTS/DISEASES	For thrips, use malathion or diazinon.
PRUNING	Prune to shape and to remove dead growth only; formal pruning is not recommended.
FERTILIZING	Apply general garden fertilizer (10-30-10) to the planting bed at 3-month intervals, and to container plants at monthly intervals. Water immediately and thoroughly after each application.
DISADVANTAGES	None.

216

Acanthaceae
(Acanthus Family)

The Greek word *akanthos* means thorn, and in this context refers to the spiny leaves borne by many of the family's species. The most famous of the plants in the group is *Acanthus mollis,* whose leaves have been stylized in the sculpture of the capitals of Corinthian columns and also are depicted in other kinds of decorative art from paintings to plaster work. In America some *Acanthus* relatives are called bear's breeches because their leaves are big, broad, and shaggy. The family includes 250 genera and about 2,500 species from many parts of the world. It is primarily a tropical and sub-tropical family composed mostly of shrubs, herbs, and vines, but very few trees.

Decorative relatives include two handsome groundcovers, snail plant *(Fittonia verschaffeltii* var. *argyroneura)* and hemigraphis *(Hemigraphis colorata).* The semiweedy, but colorful, creeping asystasia *(Asystasia gangetica)* is used often in informal hillside plantings. Another attractive near-weed is the white shrimp plant *(Nicoteba betonica),* which escapes readily from cultivation and establishes colonies along roads and on hillsides.

Adhatoda cydoniaefolia
Brazilian Bower Plant, Quince-leaved Adhatoda

As its name implies, the Brazilian bower plant is native to Brazil. It is grown only as an ornamental, although a close relative, the Malabar nut *(Adhatoda vasica),* a native of India, is used medicinally in the treatment of asthma, bronchitis, and certain other disorders, and also in the production of a yellow dye, gunpowder charcoal, and wooden jewelry. The Brazilian bower plant is prized for its handsome, large-leaved, tropical foliage, and especially for its huge clusters of flowers whose white, swan-necked blossoms are surrounded by brilliant burgundy bracts. As is the case in many members of the acanthus family, this plant's flowers are relatively small and insignificant, but are set off spectacularly by flamboyant, clustered bracts.

The Brazilian bower plant is a very large shrub, requiring an extensive garden area for a proper setting. Usually it is planted as an informal, untrimmed hedge. Its extremely dense growth provides excellent screening against visual and auditory annoyances. Most often it is chosen for the tropical appearance of its large, dark-green, prominently veined leaves and colorful flower clusters. In Hawai'i it blooms from early summer to late fall; in Brazil, during that country's winter months, July to September.

Adhatoda is a native Brazilian name for the plant; *cydoniaefolia,* from *cydonia,* meaning quince tree, and *folium,* meaning a leaf, describes the foliage as being quincelike in form.

HABIT	An erect, evergreen, woody shrub that grows to about 15 feet in height in a dense, oval crown with numerous upright branches. Large, soft, broad, oval, dark green leaves are 10 to 12 inches long; leaf veins are much depressed. Loose, cone-shaped, upright clusters of flowers rise above the foliage mass from late spring through early winter; clusters consist of many red-violet bracts surrounding small, white, tubular flowers. Small, brown fruit capsules follow. Moderately fast growth rate; easily transplanted, but it is so easily grown from cuttings that older plants are seldom moved.
GROWING CONDITIONS	Adaptable to many locations if supplied with considerable ground irrigation and protection from wind; grows best in light shade and sheltered locations; should be protected from mechanical damage caused by falling debris or strong winds.
USE	Specimen plant; mass planting; untrimmed hedge; colorful flowers; tropical effect.
PROPAGATION	May be started from seeds, but is much more easily grown from cuttings.
INSECTS/DISEASES	For Chinese rose beetles, apply one of the residual insecticides, such as carbaryl. For thrips, use diazinon or malathion.
PRUNING	Prune drastically to encourage new growth, flowering, vigorous foliage, dense crown. The best time to prune is directly after the main flowering period.
FERTILIZING	Apply general garden fertilizer (10-30-10) to the planting bed at 4-month intervals. Water immediately and thoroughly after each application.
DISADVANTAGES	Beauty of leaves is easily marred by falling debris or by strong winds.

Aphelandra sinclairiana
Coral Aphelandra

Coral aphelandra is native to the rain forests of Central America. It is one of about 80 species of the genus found growing throughout Central and South America, mainly in Brazil, Colombia, and Panama. Aphelandras as a group have little use in folk medicine or economy, but all exhibit the brilliant, cone-shaped flowers that appeal so much to gardeners. The plants also are prized for their lush tropical foliage. Some species have variegated leaves.

Coral aphelandra is a massive, tall shrub, decidedly tropical in appearance. Its large, velvety, dark green foliage creates the perfect foil for the exotic, long-lasting flower clusters, composed of velvety coral-colored bracts and brilliant cerise flowers, that appear on each branch tip. Because of its size and volume, the shrub generally is planted at the edge of a yard, where it helps to provide both screening and lush background foliage along with floral color. In Hawai'i, coral aphelandra grows best in the cool gardens of the wet upper valleys. Because its large, tender leaves are easily damaged by falling debris and heavy winds, it should be planted in protected areas.

Aphelandra, from *apheles,* meaning single, and *andro,* meaning male, refers to the single-celled construction of the male flower part; *sinclairiana* is named for Andrew Sinclair, British Royal Navy physician who made important collections of plants in South America and New Zealand.

HABIT An erect, woody, evergreen shrub that grows to about 15 feet in height in a dense, oval crown with numerous upright branches. Soft, hairy, narrow, pointed leaves are about 6 to 8 inches long. Compact, upright, cone-shaped flower clusters are about 6 to 8 inches long, each composed of many finger-like protrusions; coral-colored velvety bracts enclose the lavender-pink flowers. Blooms during summer and fall; flower clusters resemble decorations on a Christmas tree. Small brown fruit capsules follow the flowers. Moderately fast growth rate; easily transplanted, although it is so readily propagated from cuttings that older plants are seldom moved.

GROWING CONDITIONS Adaptable to many locations if supplied with considerable water and protection from wind; grows best in light shade, sheltered locations; should be protected from falling debris or winds.

USE Specimen plant; mass planting; untrimmed hedge; colorful flowers; tropical effect.

PROPAGATION May be grown from seed, but starting new plants from cuttings is much easier and faster.

INSECTS/DISEASES For Chinese rose beetles, apply one of the residual insecticides, such as carbaryl. For thrips, use diazinon or malathion.

PRUNING Prune drastically to encourage new growth, flowering, vigorous foliage, and dense crown. The best time to prune is directly after the flowering period.

FERTILIZING Apply general garden fertilizer (10-30-10) to the planting bed at 4-month intervals. Water immediately and thoroughly after each application.

DISADVANTAGES Beauty of leaves is easily marred by falling debris and strong winds.

Barleria cristata
Philippine Violet, Jhinti, Udamulli, Jhinli, Violeta,
Kolintang-violeta

The Philippine violet is not native to the Philippines, nor is it a violet. Its home is the broad subtropical region that stretches from the lower Himalayan mountains of central India, through Burma, to southern China. The Sanskrit and Bengali name for this plant is jhinti, the Tamil name is udamulli, and the Assamese name is jhinli. In India the seeds are said to have properties that make them useful antidotes for snakebites. The roots and leaves are used sometimes as poultices to reduce several kinds of swelling. A tincture made from the roots and leaves is applied to the throat to alleviate coughs. A variety of this species, *Barleria cristata* var. *dichotoma,* frequently is planted in Indian gardens and near temples. In the Philippines, where the shrub is known by its Spanish name, violeta, and also by its part Tagalog name, kolintang-violeta, it is used for ornamental hedges.

The Philippine violet is small but sprightly, its flowers bright, crisp and cheerful in appearance. It is an excellent low border plant, especially if pruned periodically to increase its bushiness. Constantly-blooming violet or white flowers are set off by small, dark green leaves. Blooming well in either full sun or light shade, this tidy plant adds brilliant spots of color to gardens the year round.

Barleria was named by Charles Plumier (1646–1704), French botanist (who is honored by the genus *Plumeria*) for Jacques Barrelier (1606–1673), French physician, botanist, plant collector, and author; *cristata,* meaning tufted or crested, refers to the crownlike green bracts at the flowers' base.

HABIT A herbaceous, sprawling, evergreen shrub that grows to about 8 feet in height and is composed of soft-textured branches and stems. Pointed, dark green leaves are about 4 inches long. Inch-long tubular flowers bloom constantly throughout the year; flowers are white, pale violet, or pale pink, with unusual hairy bracts at the base of each flower. Insignificant fruits fall to the ground, enabling plant to reseed itself. Fast growth rate; easily transplanted.

GROWING CONDITIONS Very adaptable; will grow nearly everywhere except in extreme salt conditions; prefers full sun or part shade; does well in areas of heavy rainfall, but will withstand some drought conditions.

USE Mass planting; informal hedge; colorful flowers.

PROPAGATION Grown easily from either seeds or cuttings.

INSECTS/DISEASES For thrips, apply diazinon or malathion.

PRUNING After peak flowering periods, plant should be pruned back moderately to induce new growth and vigorous flowering.

FERTILIZING Apply general garden fertilizer (10-30-10) to the planting bed at 3-month intervals. Water immediately and thoroughly after each application.

DISADVANTAGES Plant becomes rangy if not constantly cared for.

Beloperone guttata
Shrimp Plant, Flores de Camarones

Little imagination is needed to understand why almost everywhere beloperone is called the shrimp plant. The curving flower clusters, covered as they are by overlapping bracts in terra-cotta or yellow, are unmistakable shrimp-like forms. The species is native to Mexico. There, where they are called flores de camarones (shrimp flowers), and in other Central American countries, the plants grow wild along the roadsides as well as domesticated in gardens. In Hawai'i shrimp plants are used most often as colorful low hedges or borders and in mass plantings.

The species with terra-cotta bracts grows best in sunny, open locations, and will even grow at the beach if allowed a modicum of protection from the heaviest salt winds. The form with the yellow bracts is much more tender and must be planted in shady, protected locations for optimum growth. Because both color forms have a natural tendency to become lank and sparse, they should be pruned after their main flowering periods end, so that new compact and vigorous growth will develop. The plants are quite fragile, and will not stand up well against high winds or heavy garden traffic.

Beloperone, from *belos*, meaning arrow, and *perone*, meaning pointed, refers to the arrow-shaped connective tissue in the flowers: *guttata*, spotted or speckled, refers to the purple-spotted flowers nestling between the bracts.

HABIT | An erect, sometimes sprawling, evergreen shrub that grows to about 4 feet in height and has a loose crown composed of numerous soft stems and soft, pale-green leaves. Flower clusters with terra-cotta or lemon-yellow bracts are 3 to 4 inches in length, but the plant's true flowers are small, white, purple-spotted tubules almost hidden among the brilliant bracts. Not known to fruit or seed in Hawai'i. Moderate growth rate; easily transplanted.

GROWING CONDITIONS | Adaptable; will grow in moist or dry conditions with ease. The species (bearing terra-cotta bracts) grows well in full sun, even beach conditions; the form (with lemon-yellow bracts) requires shade and protection.

USE | Mass planting; container plant; flower clusters with colorful bracts.

PROPAGATION | Easily grown from cuttings of any size.

INSECTS/DISEASES | For thrips, apply diazinon or malathion.

PRUNING | Prune vigorously to induce new growth and flowering. To rejuvenate, prune back entire planting to about 6 inches above ground level; plants will send out new leaves almost immediately, and will bloom almost continuously with planned pruning.

FERTILIZING | Apply general garden fertilizer (10-30-10) to the planting bed at 3-month intervals, to container plants monthly. Water immediately and thoroughly each time.

DISADVANTAGES | Bracts of the lemon-yellow form will turn brown in strong sunlight; plants will not withstand mechanical wear and tear.

Eranthemum pulchellum
Blue Eranthemum, Limang-sugat, Guérit Petit

The blue eranthemum is native to the Philippines, Malaysia, and India. Its roots, stems, and leaves are used to heal wounds and skin ulcers in the Philippines, where it is called limang-sugat. In India a decoction of the pounded leaves is administered to treat chronic rheumatism and earache. The bitter roots are employed in China for relieving rheumatism. On the island of Réunion, in the western Indian Ocean, blue eranthemum is known as guérit petit (little cure) and is used in the treatment of infant colic.

In Hawai'i blue eranthemum generally is planted in large, low, hedgelike masses, where its deep ultramarine flowers may best be displayed. It is not an especially handsome foliage plant; here the flowers are the important feature. Constant and vigorous pruning induces dense, shrubby masses which bring forth, almost constantly, numerous flowers in a shade of blue that is not often seen in gardens.

Eranthemum, from *erranos*, meaning lovely, and *anthemon*, meaning flower, is a tribute to the flowers of the genus; *pulchellum*, meaning pretty, refers again to the blossoms.

HABIT
: An erect, woody, evergreen shrub that grows to about 6 feet in height. Its many sprawling branches are covered with dense, dark green, hairy leaves, each about 6 inches long. Erect clusters of deep ultramarine flowers rise out of green and white bracts, above the dark foliage; individual flowers are about ¾ inch in diameter. Small seed capsules follow the bloom. Plant reseeds itself readily. Moderate growth rate; easily transplanted.

GROWING CONDITIONS
: Grows best in cooler, moist locations in areas of rich, well-watered, well-drained soils. Blooms best in full sun or partial shade.

USE
: Specimen plant; mass planting; colorful flowers.

PROPAGATION
: May be propagated by seeds, but is much more easily grown from cuttings. The plant also reseeds itself.

INSECTS/DISEASES
: For spider mites, use wettable sulfur.

PRUNING
: May be severely pruned to shape and to induce new growth and flowering.

FERTILIZING
: Apply general garden fertilizer (10-30-10) to the planting bed at 3-month intervals, and to container plants at monthly intervals. Water immediately and thoroughly after each application.

DISADVANTAGES
: Seeds cast from the plant may spread it to locations where it is not wanted.

Graptophyllum pictum
Caricature Plant, Morado, Kalpueng, Ysjudemaram

This native of New Guinea is much used throughout the tropical Pacific and in the warm Asian regions as far westward as India. Filipinos know the plant as morado (meaning purple, in Spanish) or as kalpueng, one of its Tagalog names. The people of Madras State in India know the plant as ysjudemaram. In the Philippines the leaves are employed in the treatment of skin ulcers. In India the emollient leaves are applied to scorpion stings and to inflamed breasts, and the juice of the leaves is applied to cuts and dropped into the ear to relieve earache. A tonic made from the leaves is drunk sometimes to relieve constipation. In Java and the Moluccas the leaves are used to reduce swellings. In Java tricksters and magicians who chew glass chew these leaves first, leading spectators to believe that the bright red juice streaming from their mouths is blood. (For an additional use, see **Leea coccinea**).

The caricature plant is so named because of its highly varied leaf markings. No two leaves have identical designs, and each leaf appears to be hand-painted. Two common color forms are grown most often in Hawai'i; one having a green-edged leaf with white splotches at the centers and bright red veins; and the other having a yellow-edged leaf, with green splotches at the centers but without red veins. The yellow form often is confused with its near relative, the **eldorado (Pseuderanthemum reticulatum)**.

Graptophyllum, from *graptos,* meaning marked, and *phyllon,* meaning a leaf, describes the markings on the leaves; *pictum* means painted.

HABIT An erect, woody, evergreen shrub that grows to about 10 feet in height in a dense, irregular crown. Colorful, croton-like leaves of many patterns, with colors ranging from dark greens, yellows, pinks, and purples to white, are about 6 inches long and smooth, rounding to a point. Small clusters of reddish-purple flowers appear at the branch tips at intervals throughout the year. Small, club-shaped seedpods follow. Moderate growth rate; easily transplanted.

GROWING CONDITIONS Very adaptable; will grow almost anywhere except in extreme salt conditions; grows best in rich, well-watered, well-drained soil, either in the sun or partial shade.

USE Specimen plant; mass planting; container plant; colorful foliage; small but colorful flower clusters.

PROPAGATION Easily grown from cuttings.

INSECTS/DISEASES For thrips, apply diazinon or malathion.

PRUNING Prune vigorously to reduce size and to induce new growth and new foliage. Sometimes plant segments revert to forms with nonvariegated leaves. Remove the nonvariegated stem at its major connection with the root stalk.

FERTILIZING Apply general garden fertilizer (10-30-10) to the planting bed at 3-month intervals, to container plants monthly. Water immediately and thoroughly each time.

DISADVANTAGES None.

Jacobinia carnea
Jacobinia, Herva de Rato

This species of *Jacobinia*, in Portuguese-speaking Brazil, is called herva de rato (rat plant), because there the fruits of the plant are mixed with pig fat or other food material to make a bait that attracts and kills rodents. The shrub is a native of Brazil and is used primarily for decoration. Two close relatives, *J. spicigera* and *J. tinctoria*, yield blue dyestuffs similar to those of the unrelated indigos *(Indigofera suffruticosa* and *I. tinctoria)* of the bean family. Leaves of *Jacobinia spicigera*, when soaked in water, release a deep blue, nondurable dye that is used as a blueing in laundering. *J. tinctoria* yields a more durable dye. A yellow-flowered relative, *J. umbrosa*, is well known in Central and South America as monte de oro (mountain of gold).

J. carnea probably is the most popular garden plant among the 30 or so species in the genus. It was one of the first jacobinias to be included in European horticulture, having been introduced to Europe in 1827. The parent species produces pink flowers; from this, two colored forms have been developed by horticulturists, one with white blossoms, the other with deep rose flowers. This jacobinia is a small shrub generally grown in masses. Its colorful flower heads, in which each cluster is a contained group of raylike floral "spines," resemble vivid sea urchins.

Jacobinia is named for the city of Jacobina in Brazil; *carnea*, meaning fleshlike, refers to the flesh-pink flower clusters.

HABIT
: An erect, woody, evergreen shrub that grows to about 4 feet in height; its dense, rounded crown is composed of many square-stemmed branches. Large, olive-green, pointed leaves, soft and hairy, are about 12 inches long. Upright, cylindrical flower clusters appear at the branch tips, each cluster about 6 inches long; purple, pink, or white blossoms rise from rose-pink flower bracts. Not known to seed in Hawai'i. Moderate growth rate; easily transplanted.

GROWING CONDITIONS
: Very adaptable; will grow almost anywhere except in extreme salt conditions; requires constant ground moisture; grows best in rich, well-watered, well-drained soil, in sunny locations or partial shade.

USE
: Specimen plant; mass planting; low hedging; container plant; colorful flowers; tropical effect.

PROPAGATION
: Easily grown from cuttings.

INSECTS/DISEASES
: None of any importance.

PRUNING
: May be pruned judiciously to shape and to remove dead flower clusters.

FERTILIZING
: Apply general garden fertilizer (10-30-10) to the planting bed at 3-month intervals, and to container plants at monthly intervals. Water immediately and thoroughly after each application.

DISADVANTAGES
: Foliage is subject to mechanical damage from falling debris.

232

Odontonema strictum
Odontonema

Odontonema strictum, like the 40 or so other species in the genus, is native to tropical America. Among its relatives grown as ornamentals in Europe and North America are O. *barlerioides,* a red-flowered perennial from Brazil, and O. *callistachyum,* a small, red-flowered shrub from Mexico and Central America. The odontonemas appear to be purely ornamental in use, although some of their close relatives, the justicias, have certain medicinal uses. One such species, *Justicia gendarussa,* is prescribed in its native tropical Asia as a treatment for chronic rheumatism; in Réunion Island, where it is called guérit petit (little cure), as a treatment for colic; and in the Caribbean's Antilles, as a medicine for intermittent fevers.

Odontonema strictum is decidedly a tropical plant in habit and appearance. Its glossy foliage and exotic flowers create a bold jungle effect in the garden. It is an everblooming shrub whose large plumes of scarlet flowers seem to float on long, burgundy stems above the foliage. The shrub will grow easily in most Hawaiian garden locations except in the presence of salt winds. If it were able to choose its location, however, it would select the cool, moist valleys.

Odontonema, from *odonto,* meaning tooth, and *nema,* meaning thread, refers to the toothed and threadlike filaments of the flower's stamens; *strictum,* meaning drawn tight, refers to the two fertile stamens that do not protrude beyond the lip of the flower.

HABIT — An erect, herbaceous, evergreen shrub that grows to about 8 feet in height, forming multiple succulent stems and a dense crown. Glossy, dark green leaves are about 8 inches long. Erect clusters of brilliant, tubular, red flowers, each about 1 inch long, appear constantly throughout the year. Not known to fruit in Hawai'i. Fast growth rate; easily transplanted.

GROWING CONDITIONS — Very adaptable; will grow almost anywhere except in extreme salt conditions; prefers cool, moist areas, rich soil, constant ground moisture, full sun or partial shade.

USE — Specimen plant; mass planting; untrimmed hedge; colorful flowers.

PROPAGATION — Easily grown from cuttings.

INSECTS/DISEASES — For scale, apply malathion or summer oil. For thrips and mealybugs, use diazinon or malathion.

PRUNING — May be drastically pruned to reduce size and to induce new growth and flowering.

FERTILIZING — Apply general garden fertilizer (10-30-10) to the planting bed at 4-month intervals. Water immediately and thoroughly after each application. In sandy or poor soils, plant is susceptible to deficiencies of minor elements (evidenced by yellowing foliage); apply minor element fertilizers, either as foliar sprays or as soil additions, to correct this condition.

DISADVANTAGES — May become rangy if not given proper care.

234

Pachystachys lutea
Pachystachys, Lollipop Plant

This attractive plant is a recent addition to Hawai'i's flora, having been introduced to the Islands since 1970. A native of Peru, it is quite similar in appearance to the green-bracted, red-flowered cardinal's guard *(Pachystachys coccinea)* from Guyana, which has been grown in Hawai'i for several years, although it is seldom seen in Island gardens. Both plants are admired for their ornamental foliage and flowers.

P. lutea, with its bright, white-flowered spikes and butter-yellow bracts, is also quite similar in appearance to its close relative, the yellow shrimp plant, **Beloperone guttata.** Pachystachys differs from the yellow shrimp plant in that its flower spikes are decidedly erect and do not arch to the side. Moreover, its leaves are considerably larger than those of the shrimp plant. Pachystachys is an excellent choice for border beds, affording low mounds of bright yellow wherever it is planted and bringing bright color even into quite shady locations. Yet, unlike the yellow shrimp plant, it will grow and bloom abundantly in areas receiving full sun. Its perky, upright flowers bring visions of lollipops to some who view them.

Pachystachys, from *pachys,* meaning thick, large, stout (as in pachyderm), and *stachys,* meaning a spike, refers to the thick flower clusters; *lutea,* meaning yellow, describes the bright flower bracts.

HABIT
An erect, sometimes sprawling, herbaceous, evergreen shrub that grows to about 4 feet in height and forms a loose, open crown composed of numerous soft stems. Soft, somewhat hairy, pointed leaves are 6 to 7 inches long. Bright lemon-yellow, 4- to 5-inch, bracted flower clusters appear at the branch tips; several white flowers rise from the bracts at the same time, then are followed by new flowers; blossoms at intervals throughout the year, and is almost always in bloom. Club-shaped fruiting capsules with thin brown seeds follow the flowers. Moderate growth rate; easily transplanted.

GROWING CONDITIONS
Adaptable; will grow nearly anywhere except in extreme salt conditions; will grow in partial shade or full sunlight; grows best in rich, well-watered, well-drained soil.

USE
Specimen plant; mass planting; container plant; colorful bracts and flower clusters.

PROPAGATION
Easily grown from cuttings of any size, taken either from soft tender tips or from woody stems.

INSECTS/DISEASES
For thrips, apply diazinon or malathion.

PRUNING
Prune vigorously to induce new growth and flowering. With adequate pruning, plants will bloom almost constantly.

FERTILIZING
Apply general garden fertilizer (10-30-10) to the planting bed at 3-month intervals, and to container plants at monthly intervals. Water immediately and thoroughly after each application.

DISADVANTAGES
None of importance.

Pseuderanthemum carruthersii var. *atropurpureum*

Purple False Eranthemum, Purplespot Pseuderanthemum

Pseuderanthemums are often confused with their close relatives, the **eranthemums,** and therefore they've been given the prefix that makes them "false" eranthemums. The purple false eranthemum is a native of southern Polynesia, where it is commonly seen in hedges and around houses in the villages. This species is not known to have any use other than ornamental.

Purple false eranthemum is grown primarily for its foliage, even though the plant bears attractive clusters of purple flowers. The bright foliage somewhat overwhelms the flowers. The shrub exhibits two foliage forms in Hawai'i, one, purple-bronze, and the other, white-mottled gray. The plants frequently are confused with **crotons *(Codiaeum variegatum).*** However, their flowers easily differentiate them from crotons.

Eranthemum, from *erranos,* meaning lovely, and *anthemon,* meaning flower, is the name of a group of very closely related plants. *Pseuderanthemum,* from *pseudes,* meaning false, defines this plant as being not a true eranthemum; *carruthersii* may be named for William Carruthers, British botanical explorer and Keeper of Kew Gardens, 1870–1895; *atropurpureum,* is from *atro,* meaning dark, and *purpureus,* meaning purple.

HABIT
An erect, woody, evergreen shrub that grows to about 10 feet in height and has a loose, airy crown when grown in the wild; under cultivation in sunny locations, it becomes more dense. Waxy, pointed, pink and purple or gray-green and white leaves are about 6 inches long. Small purple flowers appear at the branch tips in loose, erect clusters about 6 inches in height; blooms appear almost constantly throughout the year. Flowers are followed by small club-shaped fruiting capsules, each containing 4 flat seeds. Moderate growth rate; easily transplanted.

GROWING CONDITIONS
Adaptable; will grow at the beach if protected from strong salt winds; prefers rich, well-watered, well-drained soil, but will grow in sandy locations if soil is mixed with considerable amounts of mulch or compost and if irrigation is constant; foliage of the purple form tends to fade in full, hot sunlight, and therefore it is best grown in reduced sunlight; gray-foliage form will grow well in full sunlight or partial shade.

USE
Specimen plant; mass planting; trimmed or untrimmed hedge; container plant; colorful foliage and flowers.

PROPAGATION
Easily grown from cuttings.

INSECTS/DISEASES
Thrip infestations cause the foliage colors to fade; to control, use diazinon or malathion.

PRUNING
Prune vigorously to reduce size, to induce new growth and foliage, and to produce more compact plants.

FERTILIZING
Apply general garden fertilizer (10-30-10) to the planting bed at 4-month intervals, and to container plants at monthly intervals. Water immediately and thoroughly after each application.

DISADVANTAGES
None of importance.

238

Pseuderanthemum reticulatum
Eldorado, Yellow-vein Pseuderanthemum

Eldorado is native to the open forests of Polynesia and Melanesia, where plentiful rainfall sustains the plant. When it is cultivated ornamentally in South Pacific islands, it is almost always grown as a hedge along roadsides, property boundaries, or paths leading to houses. In its natural habitat, the shaded rain forests, eldorado's growth habit is open, bordering on the straggly.

Although people often think that eldorado is a croton, inspection of its flowers should distinguish it as an acanthus. Indeed, eldorado's flowers provide an additional attraction to an already colorful plant, far surpassing as they do the modest blossoms of the crotons. It exhibits colorful, compact growth in full sunny conditions; however, if the gardener is willing to sacrifice a certain amount of compactness, eldorado will reward him with more color in shaded garden areas than most other shrubs can provide.

Eranthemum, from *erranos,* meaning lovely, and *anthemon,* meaning flower, is the name of a group of very closely related plants (p. 228). *Pseuderanthemum,* from *pseudes* (false), defines this plant as being not a true *Eranthemum;* and *reticulatum* (like a net), refers to the distinctive venation of eldorado's leaves.

HABIT An erect, woody, evergreen shrub that grows to about 6 feet in height and has a loose, airy crown when growing in the wild; under cultivation the plant tends to become more dense, probably because of pruning and availability of sunlight. Waxy, round, 4- to 5-inch leaves are pale green, yellow, and white, in varied patterns. Small white, purple-spotted flowers appear in colorful, loose, erect clusters above the branch tips continually throughout the year. Flowers are followed by small, club-shaped fruiting capsules, each containing 4 flat seeds. Moderate growth rate; easily transplanted.

GROWING CONDITIONS Adaptable; will grow at the beach if protected from strong salt winds; prefers rich, well-watered, well-drained soil, but will grow in sandy locations if soil is mixed with considerable amounts of mulch or compost and irrigation is constant; will grow well in either open sunny or partially shaded locations.

USE Specimen plant; mass planting; trimmed or untrimmed hedge; container plant; colorful foliage and flowers.

PROPAGATION Easily propagated from cuttings.

INSECTS/DISEASES None of importance.

PRUNING Prune vigorously to reduce size, to induce new growth and foliage, and to produce more compact plants.

FERTILIZING Apply general garden fertilizer (10-30-10) to the planting bed at 4-month intervals, and to container plants at monthly intervals. Water immediately and thoroughly after each application.

DISADVANTAGES None of importance.

240

Sanchezia nobilis var. *glaucophylla*
Brilliant-flowered Sanchezia

This plant was discovered in 1863, growing in the jungles of Ecuador, by an Englishman named Pearce, a collector for the Veitch Nurseries of Chelsea, England. A very colorful shrub, it is one of several *Sanchezia* species, all of which are native to tropical South America. A few horticultural varieties have been developed that show more decorative foliage than do the parent species. The sanchezias are grown for their spectacularly beautiful leaves and, to a slightly lesser extent, for their exotic flowers. Sanchezia foliage, is dramatic: individual leaves approach 18 inches in length, and cover the huge shrub with layers of variegated color. The flower clusters of *S. nobilis* combine purple, red, orange, and yellow hues in striking arrangements.

Sanchezias can become very large shrubs. Most often they are planted in large garden areas where they may best exhibit their spreading, billowing growth. Although they may be heavily pruned, the plants are much more beautiful if they are allowed to grow almost unrestrained, with only judicious pruning. They make excellent privacy screens and also introduce bright color accents in shaded locations.

Sanchezia is named for José Sanchez, nineteenth-century professor of botany at Cadiz, Spain; *nobilis,* meaning noble, describes the plant's general appearance; *glaucophylla,* from *glaucus,* meaning gleaming, and *phyllum,* meaning a leaf or petal, refers to the bright, waxy leaves.

HABIT
An erect, woody, evergreen shrub that grows to about 15 feet in height in a spreading, dense habit. Distinctive square stems support large, pointed, oval, distinctly veined leaves about 12 inches long; the veins show bright yellow in a medium green background. Erect orange, yellow, and red flower clusters about 6 to 8 inches in height appear almost constantly at branch tips. Flowers are followed by narrow seedpods, each with 6 to 8 seeds. Fast growth rate; transplantable, although cuttings provide new plants much more easily.

GROWING CONDITIONS
Adaptable; will grow almost anywhere except in extreme salt conditions; prefers cool moist areas with rich, well-watered, well-drained soil; will grow in shaded or sunny areas; must be protected from wind damage and falling debris.

USE
Specimen plant; mass planting; large untrimmed or trimmed hedges; colorful foliage and flowers.

PROPAGATION
Easily propagated from cuttings.

INSECTS/DISEASES
None of importance.

PRUNING
Prune vigorously to reduce size, to induce new growth and foliage, and to produce more compact plants.

FERTILIZING
Apply general garden fertilizer (10-30-10) to the planting bed at 4-month intervals. Water immediately and thoroughly after each application.

DISADVANTAGES
May be too large for gardens of average size.

Strobilanthes dyerianus
Persian Shield, Burma Conehead, Purple Strobilanthes

The Persian shield, a native of Malaysia and Indonesia, is one of about 250 species of *Strobilanthes,* most of which are found in Madagascar and tropical Asia. Although the Persian shield is grown primarily for its ornamental foliage, several of its relatives have some utilitarian value. The Assam indigo plant *(S. flaccidifolius),* a native of India, China, and Thailand, is the source of an important blue dye. When mixed with juice from turmeric root *(Curcuma domestica),* the dye turns green; when mixed with lime and turmeric root juice, it becomes red-brown; mixed with lime alone, the dye changes to deep blue-black; and finally, mixed with safflower seed oil *(Carthamus tinctorius),* it becomes purple. The leaves of another relative, *Strobilanthes auriculatus,* native to India, are pounded and rubbed on the body during the periods of chills in attacks of intermittent fevers, such as malaria. *S. dyerianus* was introduced into European horticulture from Burma in 1892.

The Persian shield is another acanthus endowed with vivid foliage. Its leaves exhibit the brilliance of sunlight streaming through stained glass windows. Soft and tender, they reach their greatest perfection in lush, moist, well-protected garden areas. Lavender flower clusters add an additional hue to the tinted foliage.

Strobilanthes, from *strobilos* (cone) and *anthos* (flower, bloom, or young shoot), describes the conical flower clusters; *dyerianus* is named for Sir William Turner Thiselton-Dyer (1843–1928), professor of botany at the Royal College of Science, director of Kew Gardens, and editor of *Flora Capensis* and *Flora of Tropical Africa.*

HABIT An erect, woody, evergreen shrub that grows to about 6 feet in height in a loose, airy crown. Pointed, textured, hairy, soft leaves, about 8 inches long, exhibit dark green veins with light green midrib on a purple background. Erect flower spikes support pale violet flowers; each spike about 6 inches long. Small, club-shaped capsules contain 4 flat seeds. Moderate growth rate; easily transplanted.

GROWING CONDITIONS Prefers cool, moist areas and well-watered, well-drained soil full of compost or leaf mold; requires protection from wind and sun; grows best in partial shade; thrives in areas of constant rainfall; will not grow well in hot, dry, windy areas.

USE Specimen plant; mass planting; container plant; colorful foliage.

PROPAGATION Grown easily from cuttings.

INSECTS/DISEASES None of importance.

PRUNING Prune to induce new growth and foliage and to make a more compact plant.

FERTILIZING Apply general garden fertilizer (10-30-10) to the planting bed at 3-month intervals, and to container plants at monthly intervals. Water immediately and thoroughly after each application.

DISADVANTAGES Requires a very moist, cool, protected location for optimum growth.

Thunbergiaceae
(Thunbergia Family)

The family Thunbergiaceae is named in honor of Karl Pehr Thunberg (1743–1828), one of the several naturalists whom the great botanist Linnaeus sent to different parts of the world to study and collect botanical specimens. Thunberg traveled widely in Java, Indonesia, and Japan, and ultimately returned to Sweden, where he became professor of botany at Uppsala University. The thunbergias are a small family, having only four genera and about 205 species. They were formerly classified as part of the acanthus family, but today are separated into their own distinct group. Most members of the family are tropical herbs, shrubs, and vines.

Two of the most popular species are the thunbergia vine *(Thunbergia grandiflora)*, whose pendent, blue-violet, or white flowers are seen often in Hawaiian landscaping; and the black-eyed Susan vine *(T. gregorii)*, with its brilliant orange and black flowers. (This latter plant should not be confused with another black-eyed Susan, the common, cheerful field daisy belonging to the daisy family.)

Thunbergia erecta
Bush Thunbergia

The ornamental bush thunbergia is a native of tropical West Africa. Other African relatives are employed ceremonially and in day-to-day living. Leaves of the isiphondo *(Thunbergia atriplicifolia)* are used by the Zulus as a hair-wash and as a weak enema for infants. An infusion made by soaking roots of isiphondo omkhulu *(T. venosa)* in water is drunk by a young man while he is courting, in an attempt to induce his beloved to dream of him. A similar preparation made from unohlonishwayo *(T. natalensis)* is drunk ceremonially by a bride to ensure a happy marriage.

The bush thunbergia produces bell-shaped, blue-violet flowers. It is grown in many Hawaiian gardens, generally as a specimen plant or in low hedges or borders fronting beds holding larger shrubs. Two varieties of this plant are seen less often in Island gardens: the variety *caerulea,* which bears larger flowers than does the parent species, and the variety *alba,* which produces white flowers of the same size as those of the parent.

Thunbergia is named for Karl Pehr Thunberg (1743–1828), professor of botany at Uppsala University, a student, colleague, and successor of Linnaeus; *erecta,* meaning upright, describes the plant's growth habit; *alba,* meaning white, and *caerulea,* meaning dark blue, refer to the flower colors of the two varieties.

HABIT | An erect, woody, evergreen shrub that grows to about 3 feet in height in a loose, sparse, open crown. Small, dark green leaves are about 1 inch in length. Single, dark purple or white, trumpet-shaped flowers, about 2 inches in diameter, appear constantly throughout the year. Distinctive club-shaped seed pods, split to reveal 4 rounded seeds. Moderate growth rate; easily transplanted.

GROWING CONDITIONS | Very adaptable; will grow almost anywhere except in extreme salt conditions; grows best in rich, well-watered, well-drained soils and sunny locations; becomes attenuated in shady areas.

USE | Specimen plant; mass planting; container plant; low trimmed or untrimmed hedge; colorful flowers.

PROPAGATION | Grown easily from cuttings.

INSECTS/DISEASES | For thrips, spray with diazinon or malathion.

PRUNING | Prune to reduce size, to induce new growth, foliage, and flowers, and to produce a more compact plant.

FERTILIZING | Apply general garden fertilizer (10-30-10) to the planting bed at 4-month intervals, and to container plants at monthly intervals. Water immediately and thoroughly after each application.

DISADVANTAGES | If not consistently watered, fertilized, and pruned, plant becomes unsightly.

Rubiaceae
(Coffee Family)

The term Rubiaceae is derived from the Latin word *ruber* (red) and refers to the reddish dye that is obtained from the roots of some members of the family. The dye, which is called madder in English, is produced from *Rubia tinctorum*. One of the most common madder hues is the well-known "turkey red," often used in the early years of dyeing textiles.

The coffee family is one of the largest of all plant families, having about 500 genera and 6,000 species, most of which are tropical trees, shrubs, and herbs. Several of the species maintain a myrmecophilous relationship with ant colonies (that is, an association of mutual benefit to both ants and plant).

Among the family's most important commercial crops are coffee *(Coffea arabica)* and quinine *(Cinchona officinalis)*. The noni *(Morinda citrifolia)*, a relative from the South Pacific and Southeast Asia, was brought to Hawai'i by the early Polynesian colonists, who used the bark and root as sources of dyes for tapa, and the leaves, fruits, and bark as medicinal agents. The attractive trees known as needle flower *(Posoqueria latifolia)* and wut *(Guettarda speciosa)*, and the shrubs called sweet bouvardia *(Bouvardia humboldtii)* and randia *(Randia formosa)* are grown in some Hawaiian gardens.

Coprosma baueri
Varnish Plant, Angiangi, Taupata, Mamangi, Mirror Plant,
Looking-glass Bush

Angiangi, taupata, and mamangi are Maori names for this subtropical native of northern New Zealand and its neighbors, Norfolk Island and the Kermadec and Chatham island groups. In its native habitat, the varnish plant grows as a low, prostrate shrub along the coasts and in dry rocky areas. Under more generous conditions, the plant becomes an erect tree. A close relative, *Coprosma australis,* is a New Zealand tree; its sap is used in treating some forms of skin disease, while its leaves, bark, and young shoots are employed in treating bruises, fevers, cuts, festering sores, and kidney ailments. Sometimes, too, the leaves of this tree are made into a poultice for broken limbs.

In Hawai'i the varnish plant is at its best and will bear flowers and fruits only in the cooler, higher areas, but it is also a good groundcover in seaside gardens. The plant's most attractive characteristic is its extremely shiny leaves, which gives rise to several English common names, such as varnish plant, mirror plant, and looking-glass bush. Two horticultural varieties are recognized: *marginata,* which has white-edged green leaves; and *variegata,* which has bright green leaves with golden yellow centers.

Coprosma, from *kopros,* meaning dung, and *osme,* meaning smell, refers to the foetid odor of the bruised plant; *baueri* is named for Ferdinand Bauer (1760–1826), German botanist, plant collector, and artist.

HABIT A sprawling, woody, evergreen shrub that grows to about 12 feet in height in cooler areas, much lower in warmer sections. Irregular, pendent branches are densely covered with glossy, bright green leaves 2 to 3 inches long. Plants are dioecious (that is, both male and female plants exist); tubular, insignificant, greenish white flowers appear on plants of both sexes. Reddish-orange ¼-inch fruits appear on female plants. Slow growth rate; easily transplanted.

GROWING CONDITIONS A temperate-climate plant, this *Coprosma* grows best in Hawai'i's cool or upland regions, although it will grow in a dwarfed spreading, groundcover form in lower and warmer areas. Grows best in full sun.

USE Specimen plant; mass planting; hedges at cooler elevations; groundcover at warmer elevations; container plant.

PROPAGATION Generally propagated by cuttings. Seeds are produced only at higher elevations in Hawai'i.

INSECTS/DISEASES Grasshoppers cause some minor damage; to control, spray with diazinon.

PRUNING Generally handsome when left unpruned; may be pruned vigorously into clipped hedges and other formal shapes.

FERTILIZING Apply general garden fertilizer (10-30-10) to the planting bed at 4-month intervals, and to container plants at monthly intervals. Water immediately and thoroughly after each application.

DISADVANTAGES None of any significance.

Gardenia augusta

Gardenia, Chih Tzu, Huang Chih, Kiele, Cape Jasmine, Cape Jessamine

Gardenia augusta is native to the warm temperate zones of China and Japan. The Chinese know the plant as chih tzu or huang chih (both of which mean yellow color, in reference to a vegetable dye derived from the plant). In earlier times the pulp from the fruit was an important source of yellow dye for coloring fabrics. Today, in certain areas of tropical Asia, the plant still serves as a source of the dyestuff, especially for the coloring of foods. The Malays sometimes use the leaves as poultices for sores and wounds. This plant has been grown for centuries in China and Japan as an ornamental shrub. The flowers add scent to teas and to perfumes.

A botanical variety, *radicans,* and several other horticultural varieties are sold in the nurseries; they bear such names as Mystery, Belmont, Hadley, Florida, Opera, and Fortuniana. Recently a new cultivar with variegated foliage has been introduced into Hawai'i. Some people call the parent gardenia by other names, such as cape jasmine or cape jessamine, because it resembles certain species of jasmine. The Hawaiian name is kiele.

The genus *Gardenia* is named for Alexander Garden (1730–1791), a physician in Charleston, South Carolina; *augusta* means noble or majestic.

HABIT
An erect, evergreen, woody shrub that grows to about 8 feet in height with a loose, branching crown. Large, glossy, dark green, pointed leaves are 4 to 6 inches long. Single or double flowers, velvety-white and fragrant, are 2 to 4 inches in diameter, depending on horticultural variety; blooms in late spring and early summer. Bears fruits rarely in Hawai'i. Moderate growth rate; easily transplanted.

GROWING CONDITIONS
Grows best in the cool, moist valleys and uplands; prefers rich acid soil, constant ground moisture, full sun or slight shade; not a good beach plant.

USE
Specimen plant; mass planting; container plant; fragrant blossoms.

PROPAGATION
Almost always propagated from cuttings, which will root easily even in water.

INSECTS/DISEASES
For scale and sooty mold, apply malathion or summer oil. For thrips and mealybugs, use diazinon or malathion. For oleander hawk moth caterpillars, apply one of the residual insecticides, such as carbaryl. Highly subject to nematodes.

PRUNING
May be pruned vigorously to shape and to induce new growth and flowering. Prune plants in winter to induce best spring and summer flowering.

FERTILIZING
Apply general garden fertilizer (10-30-10) to the planting bed at 2-month intervals, to container plants monthly. May be susceptible to deficiencies in minor elements (evidenced by yellowing foliage); use minor element fertilizers, to correct this condition. Must have acid soil for optimum growth; to increase soil acidity apply fertilizers prepared for acid-loving plants. The addition of epsom salts (magnesium sulfate) at the rate of 1 tsp. per 3-foot plant, scattered on the soil surface and watered in at monthly intervals, will help maintain the plant's dark green foliage.

DISADVANTAGES
Susceptible to insect damage, nematodes, and minor element deficiencies.

254

Gardenia taitensis
Tahitian Gardenia, Tiare, Tiare Tahiti, Kiele

The Tahitian gardenia is native to the Society Islands, where it is known as tiare or tiare Tahiti, and to neighboring South Pacific islands, where the beautiful shrub grows wild along the shores. Tiare blossoms are worn there as leis, in the hair, or over the ear, island-style. For special occasions, leis of these flowers are plaited into exquisite crowns for all to wear. Flowers are used also to scent coconut oil, and sometimes the blossoms are made into a medicine for easing headaches.

The Tahitian gardenia is a very popular plant in Hawai'i and one of the best for beach sites; although it will grow and bloom quite well in the wet upper valleys, it thrives best in the hot, sunny lowlands near the ocean's edge. Tiare produces large, shiny, bright green, tropical leaves that are much admired. The shrub is constantly in bloom the year round: its pinwheel flowers, intoxicatingly fragrant, scent the air by day and night. The shrub is very large, and may easily be shaped into a small tree. Tiare generally is planted in masses or as a high, informal hedge.

The genus *Gardenia* is named for Alexander Garden (1730–1791), a physician of Charleston, South Carolina, who corresponded regularly with Linnaeus; *taitensis,* meaning of Tahiti, refers to the plant's native home. Hawaiians call the plant kiele.

HABIT
An erect, woody, evergreen shrub that grows to about 18 feet in height; it is very nearly a small tree, has a dense crown, with a rather sprawling branch system. Large, glossy, dark green leaves are about 8 inches long. Single, white, velvety, fragrant pinwheel flowers, about 4 inches in diameter, appear constantly throughout the year. Bears fruits rarely in Hawai'i. Moderate growth rate; easily transplanted.

GROWING CONDITIONS
Adaptable; will grow in almost any location in Hawai'i; a good beach plant if protected from extreme salt wind; will grow in either alkaline or acid, sandy or loamy valley soils; blooms best in areas of full sun; will grow in the shade but becomes somewhat rangy, less robust.

USE
Specimen plant; mass planting; untrimmed hedge; container plant; fragrant flowers.

PROPAGATION
Usually grown from cuttings, but may be grown from airlayers.

INSECTS/DISEASES
For scale and sooty mold, apply malathion or summer oil. For thrips and mealybugs, use diazinon or malathion. For oleander hawk moth caterpillars, apply one of the residual insecticides, such as carbaryl.

PRUNING
Prune to shape and to induce new growth and flowering.

FERTILIZING
Apply general garden fertilizer (10-30-10) to the planting bed at 4-month intervals, and to container plants at monthly intervals. Water immediately and thoroughly after each application.

DISADVANTAGES
Susceptible to scale, mealybugs, and sooty mold.

Gardenia thunbergia
Tree Gardenia

The tree gardenia, native to South Africa, is found in the bush country near the Indian Ocean coast. It has several interesting uses in Africa. Several tribes, including the Zulu, take an infusion of the root bark as an emetic for biliousness. The roots, rich in tannin, are used by many African tribes to make preparations that are applied to skin lesions of leprosy. The latex is employed as a purgative. Ash from the wood is used in making soaps and dyes. The wood itself is fashioned into small utensils, clubs, ax handles, fence posts, and the like. The flowers yield an essential oil made into perfumes by the Sudanese. The fruits furnish a base for a black cosmetic. The Venda tribe use *Gardenia thunbergia* and *Dombeya rotundifolia* plants in burial ceremonies for young men who have died before marriage. Elephants, antelopes, and buffalo eat the foliage. In Florida and the Caribbean, the root stalk of the tree gardenia is the most common stock for grafting horticultural varieties of **Gardenia augusta;** it is valuable for that purpose because it is highly resistant to nematodes prevalent in that area.

This plant makes a fine tall untrimmed hedge that affords good privacy and wind screening. The flowers add scented loveliness to a garden.

Gardenia is named for Alexander Garden (1730–1791), a physician of Charleston, South Carolina, who corresponded regularly with Linnaeus; *thunbergia* is named for Karl Pehr Thunberg (1743–1828), professor of botany at Uppsala University, and both a student and successor of Linnaeus.

HABIT An erect, woody, evergreen shrub that grows to about 18 feet; almost a small tree, with loose open crown and angular branching system. Stems quite bare, foliage rather sparse. Medium green, glossy, 5-inch-long leaves are distinctively pointed, but rounded at the center. Each velvety, fragrant, pinwheel-like flower is 3 to 4 inches in diameter and has many petals on a long tubular base. Large, woody, 4-inch seedpods ripen after about 1 year on the plant. Blooms and fruits at intervals throughout the year. Moderate growth rate; easily transplanted.

GROWING CONDITIONS Very adaptable; will even grow at the beach with some protection; grows also in the cool, moist valleys, and in either alkaline or acid soils.

USE Specimen plant; small tree; fragrant white flowers.

PROPAGATION Usually grown from cuttings, but may be started from seed.

INSECTS/DISEASES For scale and sooty mold, apply summer oil or malathion. For thrips and mealybugs, use diazinon or malathion. For oleander hawk moth caterpillars, apply one of the residual insecticides, such as carbaryl.

PRUNING Prune to shape and to induce new growth and flowering.

FERTILIZING Apply general garden fertilizer (10-30-10) to the planting bed at 4-month intervals. Water immediately and thoroughly after each application.

DISADVANTAGES Susceptible to scale, mealybugs, and sooty mold.

Ixora chinensis
Ixora, Chinese Ixora, Pechah Periok, Santan-tsina,
Pōpō Lehua

Chinese ixora is native to southern China and the Malay Peninsula. Malays know the plant as pechah periok (broken cooking pot), because its angular, pointed petals resemble shards of earthenware vessels. Malays steep the root in hot water to produce a medicine used for the aftereffects of childbirth and for intestinal disorders. In India a similar tonic is said to increase gastric efficiency and is applied as a lotion to sores and skin ulcers. In the Philippines, where the plant is known by its Tagalog name, santan-tsina, the astringent flowers and roots are prepared in an alcoholic tincture for treating dysentery. And the red flowers are infused in water to make a tonic drink that, when consumed liberally, is supposed to help ward off tuberculosis and suppress certain kinds of internal hemorrhages. Ixora has also been used for centuries in the Indo-Malaysian and southern Chinese regions as an ornamental plant.

Ixora is among the most common of Hawai'i's flowering shrubs. It provides long periods of flower color, but even when not in bloom, its compact habit and dark green, glossy foliage make it an attractive landscape plant.

Ixora is from the name of a Malabar deity, Iswara, to whom the flowers of certain *Ixora* species are offered; *chinensis* means from China. Hawaiians call the several *Ixora* species pōpō lehua (meaning lehua ball), in reference to the flowers' resemblance to those of the native tree 'ōhi'a lehua.

HABIT   An erect, woody, evergreen shrub that grows to about 4 feet in height in a dense crown of multiple stems. Glossy, dark green, oval leaves are 3 to 4 inches long. Dense, rounded clusters of flowers, 4 to 5 inches in diameter, in shades of white, pink, salmon, yellow, orange, or red, bloom constantly throughout the year. Occasionally small, dark purple fruits appear. Moderate growth rate; easily transplanted.

GROWING CONDITIONS   Adaptable; will grow almost anywhere if planted in rich, well-drained, constantly moist soil; will not withstand salt winds; blooms best in sunny locations.

USE   Specimen plant; mass planting; informal hedge; colorful flowers; container plant; bonsai.

PROPAGATION   Usually grown from cuttings but may be started from seeds.

INSECTS/DISEASES   For scale and sooty mold, apply summer oil or malathion. For thrips and mealybugs, use diazinon or malathion.

PRUNING   May be pruned vigorously to shape and to induce new growth and flowering; may be trained to bonsai form.

FERTILIZING   Apply general garden fertilizer (10-30-10) to the planting bed at 2-month intervals, and to container plants at monthly intervals. Water immediately and thoroughly after each application. In sandy or poor soils, plant is susceptible to deficiencies in minor elements (evidenced by yellowing foliage); use minor element fertilizers, either as foliar sprays or as soil applications, to correct this condition.

DISADVANTAGES   Highly susceptible to insect pests, sooty mold, and deficiencies in minor elements.

Ixora odorata
Sweet Ixora, Pōpō Lehua

The beautiful sweet ixora is native to Madagascar. It is a tall shrub, almost a small tree in habit and form. Several *Ixora* species, similar in size and structure, have close-grained woods that are used for implements and in construction of small buildings. The wood of some species is so very hard that it is made into heavy-duty implements, such as pestles.

Sweet ixora is prized for its profusion of flowers during the summer and fall blooming season. The flowers are peaches-and-cream in complexion and delightfully fragrant, especially in the evening hours. If it is lighted at night, the plant is spectacularly colorful, the total effect being somewhat like fireworks against the dark sky. Sweet ixora is a tidy, naturally well-contained plant. Most often, it is grown as a specimen. However, in larger garden areas, a series of sweet ixoras makes a handsome informal hedge or background planting, provided the shrubs are pruned routinely to induce and maintain foliage near the ground.

Ixora is derived from the Sanskrit name of a Malabar deity, Iswara, to whom the flowers of certain species are offered; *odorata,* meaning fragrant, refers to the plant's nocturnal perfume. In Hawaiian all *Ixora* species are named pōpō lehua (meaning lehua ball), a reference to the flowers' resemblance to those of the native tree, 'ōhi'a lehua.

HABIT An erect, woody, evergreen shrub that grows to about 18 feet in height; it is single- or multi-stemmed, sometimes almost a small tree, with a compact, rounded crown. Glossy, dark green leaves are about 8 inches long by 2 inches wide. Large clusters of pink and cream flowers bloom during the summer and fall; individual flowers are tubular and about 6 inches long. As with other ixoras, when the plant blooms, flowers almost completely cover the plant. Not known to fruit in Hawai'i, probably because the fertilizing animal (either an insect or a bird) is not present in the Islands. Moderate growth rate; easily transplanted.

GROWING CONDITIONS Adaptable; grows best in rich, well-watered, well-drained soil and sunny locations; will grow in partial shade, but best bloom is achieved in full sun.

USE Specimen plant; large untrimmed hedge; colorful, fragrant flowers.

PROPAGATION Usually started from cuttings but may be grown from airlayers.

INSECTS/DISEASES For scale and sooty mold, apply summer oil or malathion. For thrips and mealybugs, use diazinon or malathion.

PRUNING Prune to shape; may be trained to a tree form with a single trunk or to a more shrubby effect with multiple trunks.

FERTILIZING Apply general garden fertilizer (10-30-10) to the planting bed at 4-month intervals. Water immediately and thoroughly after each application.

DISADVANTAGES Susceptible to scale, mealybugs, and sooty mold.

Mussaenda × *philippica* cv. 'Queen Sirikit'
Mussaenda Queen Sirikit

Mussaenda Queen Sirikit is a horticultural hybrid, developed in the Philippines from one parent native to those islands, kahoi-dalaga *(Mussaenda philippica)*, and the other imported from tropical Africa, Ashanti blood plant *(M. erythrophylla)*. In the Philippines, kahoi-dalaga roots and leaves are used as an antidote for snakebites and a remedy for dysentery. The crushed root is employed in the treatment of jaundice, and the leaves are incorporated into a soothing ointment. In Africa, roots of the Ashanti blood plant are eaten to whet the appetite. Other *Mussaenda* species have fragrant leaves that are used to scent clothing and hair.

Several horticultural varieties are grown in Hawai'i, among them the white-calyxed Doña Aurora (named for the wife of President Quezon of the Philippines), the pink-calyxed Doña Luz (for the wife of President Magsaysay), and the red-calyxed Doña Trining (for the wife of President Roxas). The Queen Sirikit cultivar is named for the Queen of Thailand.

Mussaenda is a Ceylonese name for several species native to that island; *philippica*, refers to that species' native habitat; *erythrophylla*, from *erythrus*, red, and *phylla*, leaves, refers to the red calices found on that species.

HABIT An erect, woody, evergreen shrub that grows to about 10 feet in height in Hawai'i (although it can become much taller in its native Philippines); has multiple stems and a bushy crown. Soft, hairy, heart-shaped leaves, about 4 to 6 inches long, are strongly marked with veins. Small, yellow-orange flowers surrounded by numerous pale pink calices bloom from spring through fall. Not known to seed in Hawai'i. Numerous horticultural varieties. Moderate growth rate; easily transplanted.

GROWING CONDITIONS Prefers hot, humid, protected jungle conditions; grows well in areas provided with extensive cloud cover or shade. Requires considerable ground moisture.

USE Specimen plant; mass planting; informal hedge; container plant; colorful bracts.

PROPAGATION Almost always grown from cuttings; sometimes propagated by airlayering. Maintain constant humidity around rooting cuttings by covering them and their container with a polyethylene bag that has a few air holes; roots form very slowly.

INSECTS/DISEASES For scale, apply malathion or summer oil. For mealybugs, use diazinon or malathion. For spider mites, spray with wettable sulfur.

PRUNING Prune to remove old flower clusters; may be pruned vigorously after blossoming season to induce new growth and flowering.

FERTILIZING Apply general garden fertilizer (10-30-10) to the planting bed at 3-month intervals, to container plants monthly. Water immediately and thoroughly. Plant is susceptible to deficiencies in minor elements (evidenced by yellowing foliage); use minor element fertilizers, as foliar sprays or as soil applications, to correct this condition.

DISADVANTAGES Will not grow well in arid places.

Pentas lanceolata
Pentas

Pentas, one of Hawai'i's most colorful flowering shrubs, is native to tropical Africa and Arabia. This everblooming plant is a constant source of vivid garden color throughout countries located in the world's cooler tropics. It is purely an ornamental plant, although its close relative, *Pentas purpurata,* has sometimes been used in the treatment of headaches, fevers, and rheumatism. Aside from its service as an ornament in the garden, pentas also provides Island flower arrangers with some of their most popular cut materials, in an assortment of whites, pinks, reds, purples, and lavenders, to be assembled in bouquets that maintain their freshness and colors for several days.

In the garden, pentas is an attractive background material, almost always planted in masses. The several color forms may be set out either in their respective color groups, so that the flower arrangers can gather them easily, or in mixed masses. Pentas improves in appearance when it is heavily pruned. Indeed, simply removing the attractive clusters of flowers invigorates the plant and induces a greater abundance of new blossoms.

Pentas, from *pente,* meaning five, refers to the fact that the several parts of a flower, such as petals and sepals, appear in arrangements of five; *lanceolata,* meaning lance-shaped or tapering at both ends, describes the shrub's leaves.

HABIT   A sprawling, woody, evergreen shrub that grows to about 4 feet in height. New growth is soft and herbaceous; many sprawling branches support a dense crown of hairy, dark green leaves. Constantly in flower throughout the year; many flower clusters, each 2 to 3 inches in diameter, appear simultaneously; colors range from white to lavenders, purples, pinks, and reds; plants grown from seeds produce new flower colors. Inconspicuous seeds appear rarely in Hawai'i. Moderately fast growth rate; older plants do not grow well when moved; new plants should be grown from cuttings.

GROWING CONDITIONS   Adaptable; grows best in cool, moist areas in well-watered, well-drained soil rich in humus; blooms well in sunny or partially shaded locations.

USE   Specimen plant; mass planting; container plant; colorful flowers; cut flowers.

PROPAGATION   Generally grown from tip cuttings; occasionally new color forms are developed from seed.

INSECTS/DISEASES   For thrips, apply diazinon or malathion. For spider mites, use wettable sulfur.

PRUNING   May be pruned vigorously to induce new growth and flowering. Plant is rejuvenated if flower clusters are consistently cut.

FERTILIZING   Apply general garden fertilizer (10-30-10) to the planting bed at 3-month intervals, and to container plants at monthly intervals. Water immediately and thoroughly after each application.

DISADVANTAGES   Relatively short-lived. New planting is necessary every 3 to 4 years.

Portlandia domingensis
Dominica Bell Flower

Although *Portlandia domingensis* is native to Dominica, a small Caribbean island near Guadeloupe, it is cultivated extensively throughout tropical America for its great beauty.

The Dominica bell flower was introduced to Hawai'i in 1934 by the U.S. Department of Agriculture. Even after so many years in the Islands, however, the Dominica bell flower is still a rare specimen plant, seldom found in local gardens. When it is seen, often it is mistakenly thought to be **angel's trumpet (Datura candida),** because of its very similar pendent flowers. This shrub's yellow-green flowers are smaller than those of angel's trumpet, but are much larger than *Portlandia grandiflora's* erect, white blossoms. A very distinctive feature of *P. domingensis* is the five triangular, flaplike lips that curve rigidly toward the interior of its flower.

The Dominica bell flower is best suited to cool, moist mountain and valley regions where rainfall is plentiful and ground moisture is certain. The shrub is extremely slow growing and difficult to transplant successfully. It is an excellent container plant, able to spend a long lifetime in a good-sized pot.

Portlandia is named for Margaret Cavendish Bentinck, Duchess of Portland (1715–1785), a student and champion of botany; *domingensis,* meaning from Dominica, refers to the plant's native habitat.

HABIT A flat-topped, spreading, woody, evergreen shrub that grows to about 12 feet in height; its horizontal branching system forms a crown that hangs to the ground; many stems can be seen amid the foliage. Glossy, leathery, gray-green, oval leaves are each about 6 inches long. Large, pendent, greenish-yellow, trumpet-shaped flowers, each about 12 inches long, appear off and on throughout the year; these spectacular blossoms hang along the branches within the crown, not from the branch tips. Not known to seed in Hawai'i. Very slow growth rate; difficult to transplant successfully.

GROWING CONDITIONS Quite adaptable; will grow in moist or dry conditions; will grow near the ocean, but cannot withstand salt winds; prefers rich, well-watered, but extremely well-drained soils; grows best in full sun, becomes ragged and rangy in the shade.

USE Specimen plant; container plant; dramatic yellow-green flowers.

PROPAGATION Quite difficult to propagate. New plants usually are started from cuttings and from seeds. Cuttings must be taken from the vertical growth at the extreme top of the plant; cuttings made from side branches will produce only rooted branches.

INSECTS/DISEASES For scale, apply summer oil or malathion.

PRUNING Prune carefully to shape only.

FERTILIZING Apply general garden fertilizer (10-30-10) to the planting bed at 3-month intervals, and to container plants at monthly intervals. Water immediately and thoroughly after each application.

DISADVANTAGES Not easily transplanted.

Portlandia grandiflora
Portlandia, Bell Flower

This exquisite portlandia is native to the Caribbean region. In Jamaica, where it is called bell flower, it grows naturally on limestone outcroppings at the base of the island's mountains. The shrub's dark brown inner bark, islanders believe, has properties similar to those of Jesuits' bark *(Cinchona officinalis)*, the source of quinine. Portlandia bark, infused in wine, is said to be an excellent soother of stomachs. A small-flowered variety, *Portlandia grandiflora* var. *parviflora*, also is widely seen in the Caribbean. Hawai'i's noted botanist Harold L. Lyon introduced the species to Hawai'i in 1928.

Somewhat reminiscent of the magnolias, this portlandia exhibits thick, glossy, leathery leaves and creamy white flowers that give off a slight fragrance. The shrub is gracefully tall and pyramidal, an attractive choice as a specimen ornamental. It is an exceptionally fine lanai plant because, once it is established in a good-sized container, it can remain there for life.

Portlandia is named for Margaret Cavendish Bentinck, Duchess of Portland (1715–1785), a student and champion of botany; *grandiflora*, from *grandis*, meaning large or great, and *floris*, meaning a flower, describes the blossoms.

HABIT An erect, woody, evergreen shrub that grows to about 18 feet in height; has an upright trunk with spreading branches and dense crown at the top of the plant. Glossy, leathery, dark green, oval leaves are about 12 inches long; foliage is very showy, making this an attractive plant even when it is not in bloom. Large, creamy white, pink-ribbed flowers, about 6 inches long and 4 inches wide, appear at intervals throughout the year; flowers stand erect from the branch tips, opening from distinctively angled, star-shaped flower buds. Plant has been known to seed on the Kona Coast of Hawai'i Island; a woody capsule, about 1 inch in diameter, opens to reveal small, dark brown, hard seeds. Very slow growth rate; difficult to transplant.

GROWING CONDITIONS Quite adaptable; will grow in moist or dry conditions; will grow near the ocean but cannot withstand salt winds; requires excellent drainage; prefers rich, well-watered, but extremely well-drained soils; performs best in full sunny conditions; becomes ragged and rangy in the shade.

USE Specimen plant; container plant; attractive white buds and flowers.

PROPAGATION Quite difficult to propagate. Cuttings must be taken from the vertical growth at the extreme top of the plant; cuttings from lower side branches will produce only rooted branches. Seeds germinate sporadically over a period of many months.

INSECTS/DISEASES For scale, apply summer oil or malathion.

PRUNING Prune carefully to shape only.

FERTILIZING Apply general garden fertilizer (10-30-10) to the planting bed at 3-month intervals, and to container plants at monthly intervals. Water immediately and thoroughly.

DISADVANTAGES Not easily transplanted.

Rondeletia amoena
Rondeletia, Yellowthroat Rondeletia

This everblooming shrub is indigenous to the part of the American isthmus that stretches from southern Mexico to Colombia. Rondeletia is purely an ornamental plant, even though it is a member of the highly utilitarian coffee family. Although its near relative *Rondeletia odorata* has a lovely fragrance, *R. amoena* is odorless. The sprightly shrub makes up for this shortcoming through a constant display of masses of highly colorful flowers. Rondeletia's very dark green foliage effectively sets off the plant's brilliant clusters of red-orange and yellow flowers. The blossoms themselves are distinctive in that their centers appear to be made of small golden rings. This characteristic has led gardeners to call the plant yellowthroat rondeletia.

Sometimes rondeletia is grown as a specimen, but most often it is planted in informal mounding masses in much the same way as is the look-alike, but unrelated, **lantana *(Lantana camara)***. Rondeletia does not suffer from the insects that have been imported to eradicate wild lantana plants. It thrives in dry, sunny locations and makes a very colorful container plant on a sunny terrace or lanai.

Rondeletia was named by Charles Plumier (1646–1704), French botanist (after whom *Plumeria* was named) for Guillaume Rondelet (1507–1566), chancellor of the University of Montpelier, France, a physician and naturalist; *amoena* means charming, delightful, or lovely.

HABIT	An erect, oval-headed, woody, evergreen shrub that grows to about 10 feet in height and forms a dense crown with branches to the ground. Hairy, oval, medium green leaves are about 3 inches long, rather convex in form. Showy, compact clusters of apricot-orange and yellow flowers are about 4 inches in diameter; individual flowers are slightly trumpet-shaped, about ½ inch in diameter; blooms constantly throughout the year. Not known to seed in Hawai'i. Moderate growth rate; easily transplanted.
GROWING CONDITIONS	Very adaptable; will grow almost anywhere except in extreme salt conditions; prefers rich, well-watered, well-drained soil; grows and blooms best in full sun; becomes ragged and rangy in the shade.
USE	Specimen plant; mass planting; trimmed or untrimmed container plant or hedge; low border plantings; colorful flowers.
PROPAGATION	Easily grown from cuttings.
INSECTS/DISEASES	For scale, apply summer oil or malathion. For thrips and mealybugs, use diazinon or malathion.
PRUNING	May be pruned vigorously to shape and to induce new growth and flowering.
FERTILIZING	Apply general garden fertilizer (10-30-10) to the planting bed at 3-month intervals, and to container plants monthly. Water immediately and thoroughly each time.
DISADVANTAGES	Susceptible to several insect pests.

Serissa foetida
Serissa, Hakuchoge, Kao tawk

This serissa is native to southern Japan, Formosa, China, and Southeast Asia. In Japan, where it is one of the most important of ornamental plants, the little shrub is called hakuchoge (white bird feathers) because of the feathery white flowers. Japanese will plant hakuchoge singly or in small groups in their gardens, alongside rocks or near streams and pathways. Both the Chinese and Japanese use it for low, clipped hedges, in much the same way as boxwood is employed in Europe and America. The Chinese believe that the root possesses medicinal virtues and use the leaves and stems in treating carbuncles and certain kinds of cancers. The Thais use the plant ornamentally, calling it kao tawk (left over cooked rice) because of the shape of the flower petals.

Usually serissa is treated as a bonsai plant in Hawai'i. Oftentimes gardeners will thin the foliage by artful pruning in order to show its handsome trunk and branches. In Japan, in contrast, the shrub generally is pruned to create dense, mounded forms that look like rounded, growing stones. Either style of pruning works well for Hawaiian gardens. Serissa is a small-scale plant with tiny variegated green and white leaves, and white flowers that are scarcely larger. It is handsomely displayed in the garden either singly or in masses. In addition, it is an attractive container plant for terrace or lanai.

Serissa is the latinized spelling of an Indian name for the plant; *foetida*, meaning stinking or malodorous, refers to the foul odor that is released when the branches are bruised.

HABIT A low, spreading, bushy, woody, evergreen plant that grows to about 3 feet in height in a naturally compact, dense crown. Small, glossy, dark green leaves with white-banded edges are about ¼ inch long. Small, white, single or double flowers, about ½ inch in diameter, appear during spring, summer, and fall. Not known to fruit in Hawai'i. Slow growth rate; easily transplanted.

GROWING CONDITIONS Adaptable; will grow in almost any location except in extreme salt conditions; will grow in either full sun or partial shade; prefers rich, well-watered, well-drained soil.

USE Specimen plant; low hedge; mass planting; container plant; bonsai; small white flowers.

PROPAGATION Very easily grown from cuttings.

INSECTS/DISEASES None of importance.

PRUNING Easily pruned to shape and to induce new growth, compactness, and flowers.

FERTILIZING Apply general garden fertilizer (10-30-10) to the planting bed at 3-month intervals, and to container plants at monthly intervals. Water immediately and thoroughly after each application.

DISADVANTAGES Overwatering in poor soils will cause the plant to die.

Caprifoliaceae
(Honeysuckle Family)

An old European name for honeysuckle is caprifolium, a word derived from the Latin word *caper,* meaning goat. This appellation may refer to the fact that the flower buds of some species resemble the curved horns of goats. Twelve genera and about 450 species comprise the family, and most of those are trees and vines native to the Earth's temperate and tropical mountain regions.

The elderberry *(Sambucus canadensis)* bears the well-known edible fruit that provides excellent fillings for pies and, when properly fermented, a flavorful wine. Probably the family's most common garden plant is the honeysuckle *(Lonicera japonica).* Other decorative relatives are sweet viburnum *(Viburnum odoratissimum)* and snowball bush *(V. tomentosum).*

Abelia × *grandiflora*
Glossy Abelia

The glossy abelia is a horticultural offspring of two matt-leaved species native to China, *Abelia chinensis* and *A. uniflora.* The parents, usually seen in the wild and not especially suitable for use in gardens, have produced an attractive offspring that is often grown in temperate gardens. Most of the abelias have little use other than their natural visual value in the landscape. A more famous relative, *Lonicera japonica,* one of the common honeysuckles we all know, has the decorative value and delicate fragrance associated with the group. In addition, its leaves contain an efficient laxative and its stems are fibrous enough to permit their use in basketry and plaiting.

Glossy abelias produce graceful, bell-shaped flowers that usually appear in pairs. The flowers exude a perfume that is the essence of spring, even in Hawai'i, where they bloom during most of the year. Hawai'i's semitropical climate forces the plants into periods of extended bloom, warring against the biological dictates established by rigorous seasonal cycles in the Asian climes of their origin.

The abelias are essentially background plants, best set off at the sides and in corners of gardens, where their crisp flowers may be appreciated at a distance, and where their almost flawless, small-scale foliage may provide subdued settings for more spectacular foliar and floral displays.

Abelia is named in honor of Clarke Abel (1780–1826), a physician to the British Embassy in China in 1817, author of *Narrative of a Journey into China;* and *grandiflora,* from *grandis,* large, and *floris,* a flower, describes the size of this plant's flowers relative to those of other abelias.

HABIT | An erect, woody, evergreen shrub that grows to about 8 feet in height with multiple spreading branches. Glossy, dark green leaves are about 1 inch long; new foliar growth is reddish. Pinkish white, bell-shaped flowers, in hanging clusters along the branches, appear at intervals throughout the year; each flower is about ½ inch in diameter. Not known to fruit in Hawai'i. Moderate growth rate; easily transplanted.

GROWING CONDITIONS | Very adaptable; will grow nearly anywhere in Hawai'i except in extreme salt exposures; prefers cool, moist areas, full sun or partial shade.

USE | Specimen plant; mass planting; formal and informal hedges; bright, springlike flowers.

PROPAGATION | Almost always grown from cuttings in Hawai'i.

INSECTS/DISEASES | For thrips, use diazinon or malathion.

PRUNING | May be vigorously pruned to shape; easily pruned into formal hedges, topiary, and espalier forms; tends to become rangy if unpruned.

FERTILIZING | Apply general garden fertilizer (10-30-10) to the planting bed at 3-month intervals. Water immediately and thoroughly after each application.

DISADVANTAGES | Requires more than the usual amount of pruning to maintain a compact form.

Appendix 1
Insect Pests and Plant Diseases

Sucking Insects

SCALE INSECTS There are several kinds of scale insects; the species most commonly found in Hawaiʻi are the green scale, white armored scale, red wax scale, and barnacle scale. These insects live by sucking nutrients from the leaves, stems, and branches of the many susceptible plants. The actual insect lives protected in its familiar round or flattened, disklike cover attached securely to the plant tissue. These covers may be brown, black, white, green, or pink in color.

Control scale by spraying malathion in 2 applications, 14 days apart, on the upper and lower surfaces of the foliage and on the stems and branches. Natural biological control is provided by ladybird beetles, which feed on these insects.

Scale insects exude a honeydew that attracts ants, which then become a pest, and also provides nourishment for sooty mold (a fungus). To control ants, apply malathion or diazinon to the plant's base. To eradicate or prevent sooty mold, the scale insects must be controlled.

MEALYBUGS Mealybugs are closely related to the scale insects. They are curiously shaped, white-coated insects that resemble slow-moving pieces of waxy cotton lint. They are generally found in colonies on the surfaces of the leaves, stems, branches, and roots of many Island plants. Several generations are produced during the course of a year. They feed by sucking nutrients from the plant tissue.

Control mealybugs by applying diazinon or malathion sprays in 2 treatments, 14 days apart, to the upper and lower surfaces of the leaves and to the stems and branches. Drench the surrounding soil with the same insecticides if mealybugs have attacked the plant's roots.

Mealybugs exude a honeydew that attracts ants, which then become a pest, and also provides nourishment for sooty mold (a fungus). To control ants, apply malathion or diazinon to the plant's base. To eradicate or prevent sooty mold, the mealybugs must be controlled.

THRIPS Several species of thrips are found in Hawaiʻi; some of them attack only certain plant species. They are particularly attracted to gardenia flowers and Chinese banyans. Thrips are small, slender, shiny black insects that appear in considerable numbers. A characteristic feature is that they raise their tails in a menacing attitude as if to sting (which they are not capable of doing). These insects live by sucking sap from the plant's flowers, leaves, and stems. Damage to the plant consists of malformed or unopened flower buds and lackluster, curled leaves. The foliage often turns silvery from the rasping, sucking, feeding action of the insects.

Control thrips by applying diazinon or malathion in 2 treatments, 14 days apart, to the upper and lower surfaces of the flowers and leaves, and to the branches.

APHIDS These are small, soft, dull-colored insects that appear in dense clusters along the stems, leaves, buds, and flowers of many plants. Sometimes plant parts are almost completely covered by multitudes of these insects. They feed by sucking out the sap, which deforms buds, pits fruits and vegetables, and discolors and curls foliage. Numerous generations are produced throughout the year. Some adults develop wings, which allow them to fly to new feeding areas.

Control aphids by applying dimethoate, diazinon, or malathion spray in 2 treatments, 14 days apart, to the upper and lower surfaces of the foliage, to flowers, and to the stems and branches. Aphids exude a honeydew that provides nourishment for sooty mold (a fungus), which is controlled by eradicating the aphids. Ants use the aphids as cattle, milking the honeydew from the aphids' bodies. Control ants by applying malathion or diazinon to the plant's base. Aphids are carriers of several virus diseases, such as the dread papaya mosaic virus. Eradication of aphids is one of several control measures for virus diseases.

SOUTHERN GREEN STINKBUGS These are the unwelcome, shield-shaped, green or bronze-green insects that produce a highly offensive odor when pinched or stepped on. They live by sucking sap from the leaves, stems, and fruits of many plant species, causing deformed leaves, stems, and fruits. Often the plant tissue becomes infected at the hole where the insect has fed, causing a rotten fissure to develop.

Control this pest by applying diazinon or malathion sprays in 2 treatments, 14 days apart, to the upper and lower surfaces of the foliage and to the branches and fruit. Two beneficial insects have been introduced in Hawai'i to prey (as parasites) on the southern green stinkbug—an effective biological control.

SPIDER MITES These tiny creatures are true spiders that live in multitudinous colonies on the flowers, leaves, and stems of many plants. Spider mites are so small that they can usually be seen only under a magnifying glass. Damage to the plant is the visual evidence that the mites are present. These creatures suck the sap from plant tissues, causing discolored and deformed leaves and flowers. Often the foliage turns a listless yellow and the leaves curl; fruits are left with a russet, scaly scar where the spiders have fed.

Control spider mites by applying wettable sulfur or kelthane sprays in 2 treatments, 14 days apart, to the upper and lower surfaces of leaves and to stems, branches, flowers, and fruits. Damage to fruit may be prevented by spraying the plant just after the main flowering period when the fruit begins to form. To protect the leaves from attack, the chemical should be applied during the time when the new foliage appears.

Chewing Insects

CHINESE ROSE BEETLES These beetles are among the most voracious and destructive chewing pests in Hawai'i, feeding on many Island plants. They are more commonly found in the hot, dry Island areas than in the cooler, moister sections. The tan-colored, oval-shaped adult beetles are about ¼-inch in length. They fly readily, hide during the day under dry plant litter, and emerge at dusk to feed until nearly midnight. They will not feed during daylight hours or at night if plantings are well lighted. The insect feeds on the central portions of a plant's leaves (not along the edges) and may cause extremely heavy damage, making lacework of the foliage. Tender, large-leaved plants, such as the acalyphas, gingers, heliconias, mountain apple, grapes, avocados, and false kamani, are particularly susceptible to Chinese rose beetle attack.

Control this pest by applying one of the residual insecticides, such as carbaryl, in 2 treatments, 14 days apart, to the upper and lower surfaces of the foliage. Control is aided by keeping the garden area clear of all fallen leaves, debris, and compost, so that the insects cannot hide and breed among the ground litter. It is also helpful to light susceptible plants artificially during the feeding hours.

GRASSHOPPERS Several grasshopper species, easily identified by their unique shapes, are found in Hawaiian gardens. Like Chinese rose beetles, these pests inflict severe damage on many garden plants. Damage from grasshoppers is easily distinguished from that of rose beetles, for grasshoppers begin chewing at the outer margin of the leaf rather than at the center. They are seldom seen feeding, as they fly away from the leaves after taking their fill.

Grasshoppers may be controlled by applying one of the residual insecticides, such as carbaryl or dursban, in 2 treatments, 14 days apart, to the upper and lower surfaces of the foliage.

CATERPILLARS Several destructive moth and butterfly caterpillars are common in Hawaiian gardens. Some of these are the large oleander hawk moth, citrus swallowtail butterfly, monarch butterfly, and various smaller moths. The caterpillars may devour much of a plant's foliage overnight, and also may badly damage some flowers and flower buds (unopened flower buds of hibiscus, crown flowers, and geraniums are particularly susceptible).

To control the various moth and butterfly caterpillars, apply one of the residual insecticides, such as carbaryl, in 2 treatments, 14 days apart, to the upper and lower surfaces of the leaves and to the buds and flowers.

Other Infestations and Diseases

SOOTY MOLD This fungus disease is characterized by a black, sooty covering on various parts of many plant species. It lives on the honeydew secreted by scale insects, mealybugs, aphids, and whiteflies. Excessive growth of sooty mold is deleterious to the plant in that it interferes with photosynthesis; the leaves weaken and ultimately shrivel.

To control sooty mold, the insects that produce the honeydew must be eradicated. Lack of honeydew causes the fungus to roll up like sunburned skin and drop from the plant.

LEAF SPOT DISEASES Brown, dead spots appear on the leaves of many Hawaiian plants. The exact cause of a particular case of leaf spot is difficult for any but a plant disease expert to determine, as any of several different organisms may be responsible.

Leaf spot due to rust fungus on roses (common during wet weather) may be controlled by weekly applications of the zineb form of maneb. For other leaf spot diseases, common to many Island plants, apply tri-basic copper sulfate spray at weekly intervals until the disease is controlled.

POWDERY MILDEW This disease is easily identified by its talcum-like appearance on the foliage, stems, and flower buds of several plant species. It is especially common on roses, acalyphas, and hydrangeas, but also afflicts many vegetables and other soft, herbaceous plants. It is most often seen during periods of damp weather. Control powdery mildew by 2 applications of powdered or wettable sulfur or liquid mildew fungicide, 14 days apart, on the upper and lower surfaces of the leaves, stems, and flower buds.

NEMATODES More than 25,000 species of these tiny eel worms are known throughout the world. Some of them attack plant roots, sucking nutrients from the tissues. Damage is so severe, often resulting in greatly deformed, almost cancer-like root development, that the roots are unable to carry out their nutrient-gathering functions for the growing plant. Evidence of nematode infestation may be seen by inspecting visually the plant's roots. An above-ground symptom is severe wilting of plants during the heat of the day, even when the surrounding soil is moist, because the roots are unable to absorb enough moisture to keep the plant supplied during the warm, dry period. The presence of nematodes is also suspected when patches of unhealthy plants appear in otherwise healthy plantings.

Nematode attack can be prevented by selecting resistant varieties (e.g., local Hawaiian tomatoes are bred for resistance to nematodes). Soil nematodes can be eliminated only by fumigating the planting soil where they are present; this process should be undertaken only by experienced fumigators authorized by the Hawaii State Department of Agriculture. For potted plants, use sterilized potting soil. Do not put into the soil new plants that show any sign of attack by nematodes. The healthy tops of diseased plants may be used for propagation and their roots dug up and destroyed. All plant material that shows evidence of nematode attack should be destroyed.

Appendix 2
Plant Propagation

CUTTINGS Dip the cut ends of 4-inch-long stem cuttings, with half the leaves removed, in growth regulator, and plant in vermiculite or perlite. Place container in a partially shaded location, and keep lightly moist. When cuttings are well rooted, transplant to a permanent garden site.

SEEDS Remove ripe seeds from pods and fleshy seedcoats and, for best results, plant immediately. Sprinkle soil lightly over seeds in a bed of well-drained potting soil; cover seeds to a depth approximating the dimension of their diameters; tiny, dustlike seeds are generally scattered on the soil surface and left uncovered. Keep the seedbed lightly moist. Seeds usually germinate over a period of several weeks, although those of a few species may take months to sprout. Transplant seedlings to permanent garden locations when they reach 2 or more inches in height and have developed at least a half dozen mature leaves.

ROOT DIVISION Clumping plants are easily propagated by root division. Remove rooted offshoots from the main root mass by severing with a sharp knife or by lifting the entire root mass and dividing the clump into several sections by cutting or pulling apart. Transplant divisions to protected garden locations and keep constantly moist. Most divided plants adapt readily to new garden sites. Do not fertilize new plants until they show vigorous new foliar growth.

GRAFTING Plants are often propagated by grafting in order to preserve established varieties and to obtain strong-rooted plants from otherwise weak-rooted cutting material. Some plants, such as the many hibiscus hybrids, have inherently weak roots; grafting allows the weak-rooted but desirable hybrids to be established on stronger and more vigorous rooted stock. The process may be done in several ways, the most common of which is the "side graft," which is described here.

In this process a cutting (scion) of a desired plant is imbedded into the stem of a strong-rooted relative in such a way that the growing surfaces of both scion and rootstock are pressed together to allow the tissues to heal and grow together. Generally, the rootstock is about ¾ inch in diameter and the scion, slightly smaller. Cut the base of a 3-inch length of the scion into a 2-sided sharp wedge and insert it into a diagonal gash cut about a quarter of the way through the diameter of the stock. Seal the junction with plastic tape or raffia covered with melted paraffin. The graft should begin to produce new foliage within about 4 months. After the scion shows vigorous growth, prune off all rootstock growth directly above the graft, and seal the cut with a tree pruning compound. This allows the graft to be established as the sole crown of the plant. As the plant grows, keep all sucker growth removed from below the graft union so that the rootstock cannot overwhelm the graft.

AIRLAYERING New plants may be made to form on the branches and trunks of established woody shrubs by inducing them to sprout roots. This process is called airlayering. First, make two parallel cuts through the bark, completely around a ½-inch-diameter branch or stem; the cuts should be one inch apart. Remove the bark between the two cuts, laying the wood beneath bare. Apply a small amount of growth regulator to the stem section where the bark has been removed. Cover the cut surface with a handful of dampened but not overly wet sphagnum moss. Cover the dampened moss with a small rectangle of polyethylene plastic sheeting, and tie securely at both edges of the plastic so that the moss is completely wrapped and covered. Be sure that the ends of the plastic overlap at the seam so that the moistened moss is firmly contained. Roots develop along the cut surface within about 4 months' time. The roots, when well developed, can be easily seen through the transparent plastic sheeting.

When well rooted, sever the branch from the parent plant and discard the plastic cover. At the time of separation from the parent, remove about a third of the foliage from the airlayered branch to prevent wilting. Set the rooted airlayer in extremely well drained potting soil, and stake it firmly upright to hold it in place. Set the potted airlayer in a partially shaded location for approximately one month. Then in a sunnier area for 2 weeks before setting it out in the permanent garden location.

Index of Plant Names

287

Index